Briefcase on Company Law

Joanna Gray, LLB, LLM (Yale), Solicitor
Lecturer in Law, University of Newcastle Upon Tyne,
Senior Research Fellow in company and
commercial laws, Institute of Advanced Legal Studies,
University of London

First published in Great Britain 1997 by Cavendish Publishing Limited
The Glass House, Wharton Street, London, WC1X 9PX

Telephone: 0171-278 8000 Facsimile: 0171-278 8080

Gray, Joanna
Company law. – (Briefcase Series)
I. Title II. Series
344.10666

ISBN 1 85941 242 4

Printed and bound in Great Britain

Acknowledgments

I would like to thank Adrian Hoggarth and Kate Dawson for help in the preparation of Parts 2 and 4.

Contents

Part 3: Corporate finance

Part 4: Insolvency

Table of Cases

Table of Statutes

1 Corporate personality

1.1 Doctrine of corporate personality

Salomon v A Salomon & Co Ltd (1897) HL

The appellant, Mr Salomon, was a boot manufacturer in the East End of London. He had been a successful sole trader for over 30 years. The respondent company was formed to purchase and take over the business of Mr Salomon with seven subscribers (the requisite statutory minimum in those days). These subscribers were Mr Salomon who owned 94 of the shares and six members of his family who owned one share each as nominees for Mr Salomon. The purchase price for Mr Salomon's business was £39,000. Mr Salomon was to receive £20,000 out of future profits as they came into the company but he took this sum in the form of £10,000 worth of fully paid shares in the company and a debenture worth £10,000 secured over the company. The balance of the purchase price was made up by the company's discharge of the sole tradership's debts and liabilities at the time of its transfer. During the year after its incorporation the new company encountered trading difficulties. The appellant attempted to keep the company going by lending it money raised by way of a mortgage of his debenture but it was to no avail and the company went into liquidation. When the mortgagee of the debenture brought enforcement proceedings, the liquidator argued that the debenture was invalid as it had been originally obtained through the appellant's 'fraud', in the sense that the formation of what was in effect a one man company amounted to a fraud. The court at first instance and the Court of Appeal found for the liquidator in that they refused to recognise the existence of A Salomon & Co Ltd as a separate legal person. They saw the company as nothing more than Mr Salomon's nominee, agent or trustee.

Held On appeal, the House of Lords unanimously reversed the findings of the lower courts. Lord Halsbury LC said that so long as the statutory formalities for forming and registering an incorporated company had been complied with (and they had) then the motive of those forming a company was irrelevant to the question of its existence as a legal person separate from its members. It makes no difference to this rule that one member owns the beneficial interest in all or substantially all of the company's shares. The company exists at law and is a being entirely separate from those who own its shares or run its business.

Macaura v Northern Assurance Co (1925) HL

The appellant, Mr Macaura, owned several timber estates in Ireland. He sold them to a company in return for the allotment to him of nearly all of the company's share capital, the remainder of the company's share being held by nominees for his benefit. He was a also a substantial creditor of the company. Insurance policies were effected covering the timber in his name. When fire subsequently ravaged the timber he brought an insurance claim on the policies.

Held The claim failed. He had no insurable interest in the timber. The timber was the property of the company not of him; this was a consequence of its separate legal personality. The fact that Macaura was the only beneficial shareholder in the company and was its major creditor (so that he had a very real economic interest in the timber) made no difference for it was not his shares or the debt owed him which were exposed to the fire, it was the timber and that was the property of the company.

Lee v Lee's Air Farming Ltd (1961) PC

The appellant was the widow of Mr Lee, sole director and holder of 2,999 of the 3,000 shares in the respondent company. He had been employed by the company too and was killed in an accident in the course of his employment. The question arose as to whether he was a 'worker' for the company within the meaning of New Zealand worker compensation legislation, in which case his widow was entitled to compensation from the company. The New Zealand Court of Appeal had ruled that he was not since he was *de facto* also the employer in that for all intents and purposes he really was the company.

Held The appeal was allowed. It was a necessary consequence of the separate legal personality of the company that contractual relations could exist between the deceased Mr Lee and the company. They were two separate legal entities and there was nothing to prevent the person who is in sole control of a company from, at the same time, being employed by it.

1.2   Lifting the veil of incorporation

1.2.1   Fraud

Gilford Motor Co v Horne (1933) CA

The respondent, Mr Horne, had contracted with the appellant, the Gilford Motor Company, not to solicit its business customers when he left its employment. After he had ceased to work for the appellant, Mr Horne formed a company which carried on a competing business and began to solicit the appellant's customers. Mr Horne was neither a director nor a shareholder in this company – his wife and an employee of the company (who, incidentally, called Mr Horne 'Boss'!) were the only directors and shareholders.

Held An injunction to restrain further breaches of Mr Horne's covenant was granted against both Mr Horne and the new company. The Court of Appeal saw the company as nothing more than a sham, a stratagem to circumvent the covenant to which Mr Horne was a party. Mr Horne was effectively carrying on business through the agency of this company.

Jones v Lipman (1962)

The defendant had contracted to sell land to the plaintiff. The defendant was now trying to prevent the plaintiff obtaining specific performance of the contract so he conveyed the land to a company formed for this express purpose and owned and controlled by him. The defendant argued that the company, as a separate legal person, was a *bona fide* purchaser for value without notice of the land and so specific performance could not now be ordered over the land.

Held The judge ignored the corporate veil for the purposes of the defendant's argument. He followed the reasoning in *Gilford v Horne* and ordered specific performance against both the defendant and the company which now held the land.

Re H and others (restraint order: realisable property) (1996) CA

One hundred per cent of the shares in two family companies were owned by the three individual defendants in this action, and a fourth individual who intervened in the proceedings. The three defendants were the subject of proceedings brought against them by the Commissioners of Customs and Excise relating to excise duty fraud allegedly committed by the defendants through the companies. The Commissioners had obtained orders restraining the defendants from dealing with their realisable property. A receiver was appointed over the property concerned which included shares in the two family companies and motor vehicles and stock belonging to the companies. The defendants and intervenor appealed against the terms of the order arguing that it infringed the principle of separate corporate personality and that the company's assets were being wrongly treated as their assets.

Held The Court of Appeal rejected the appeal holding that this was an appropriate case for lifting the veil of incorporation of the companies concerned and treating their assets as inuring to the defendants personally. The evidence pointed to the use of the corporate form as a masquerade for illegal and criminal activities (evasion of excise duty) – the companies were controlled by the defendants who had benefited substantially from

3

company money. Following the *dicta* in *Adams v Cape Industries plc*, 'the court will lift the corporate veil where a defendant by the device of a corporate structure attempts to evade (i) limitations imposed on his conduct by law ...'. The Court of Appeal affirmed the orders made which treated the companies' assets as belonging to the defendants.

1.2.2 Groups of companies

DHN-Food Distributors Ltd v Tower Hamlets London Borough Council (1976) CA

DHN Food Distributors Ltd, the parent company in the DHN group, owned and ran a food distribution business. It wholly owned two subsidiary companies: Bronze Investments Ltd (which owned the land used in the business) and DHN Food Transport Ltd (which owned the lorries). The same directors were common to all three companies. The local authority issued a compulsory purchase order over the land pursuant to which statutory compensation was payable for (1) the value of the land, and (2) disturbance to any business conducted. The local authority paid compensation for the land value to Bronze Investments Ltd but nothing at all with respect to business disturbance since it did not own or carry on any business. The parent company owned and carried on the business but was separate in law and was not subject to the compulsory purchase order and hence, argued the local authority relying on the doctrine of separate corporate legal personality, not entitled to any compensation at all.

Held The Court of Appeal thought this an artificial and unfair application of the doctrine of corporate personality. Lord Denning lifted the corporate veil and said that compensation for business disruption should be payable to DHN Food Distributors Ltd. He treated the group as one entity for the purposes of that particular statute. This decision was carefully confined to its facts and does not lay down any principle generally applicable in group situations.

Lonrho Ltd v Shell Petroleum Co Ltd (1982) HL

The appellant company, Lonrho Ltd, had brought an action for discovery of documents which it claimed were under the control and in the power of the respondents in that they were held by overseas subsidiary companies wholly owned and controlled by the respondents.

Held The appeal was disallowed and Lonrho's action failed. The House of Lords restated the strict principle that even within seemingly closely interconnected groups of companies the individual companies still enjoy separate corporate personality in law and the courts will not lightly disregard that and set aside the veil of incorporation. However, they did leave open the possibility of doing so where the facts show that a company is completely subservient and totally compliant with the wishes and demands of another person.

Adams v Cape Industries plc (1990) CA

The plaintiffs had a judgment awarded in a Texas court against the defendant company's US subsidiary. The plaintiffs were now seeking to enforce it against the assets of all companies in the Cape Industries group worldwide.

Held The attempt at enforcement failed. The Court of Appeal said that just because the commercial direction and policy of the subsidiary company was dictated by the group does not mean that the subsidiary company is a dependent entity at law. It was an independent company with capacity to enter into its own contracts and run its own business.

Re Polly Peck International plc (in administration) (1995)

PPIF was a wholly owned subsidiary of Polly Peck International ('PPI') and had been set up to raise finance for the whole Polly Peck group of companies by making bond issues. This it did and the bonds expressed that PPI guaranteed PPIF's obligations under the bonds, and that PPI could be substituted for PPIF as the principal debtor under the bonds. All the money received by PPIF from these bond issues was loaned in turn to PPI. PPIF did not even have its own bank current account and payments due under the bonds, and costs associated with them, were paid by PPI. PPI went into administration and a scheme of arrangement was eventually concluded, the terms of which precluded a creditor obtaining payment twice in respect of the same claim.

At around the same time this scheme of arrangement was concluded, PPIF went into voluntary liquidation and the bondholders claimed sums owing on the bonds against PPI pursuant to the guarantees it had given when PPIF issued the bonds. Since the monies raised by the bonds had been loaned in turn by PPIF to PPI, the liquidator of PPIF claimed against PPI in respect of that loan. The question for the court was whether to treat PPI and PPIF as in effect the same entity and therefore see these two claims as being in respect of the same obligation, and therefore excluded by the scheme of arrangement's rule against double recovery. Or should the court respect PPIF's *de jure* separate existence and see its claim against PPI as separate and distinguishable from that of the bondholders'?

Held The court refused to disregard the principle of separate corporate personality and disallow the claim by PPIF's liquidator against PPI. It said it must look to the legal form of the transactions that took place rather than their economic substance and PPIF could not be regarded as acting as a mere agent of PPI. Neither should it be aggregated with PPI into one single economic entity – there were no grounds to set aside its veil of incorporation and so both claims arising from the PPI group's bond issue were admitted.

1.2.3   Public policy

Daimler Co Ltd v Continental Tyre and Rubber Co (GB) Ltd (1916) HL

The respondent company was incorporated in England in order to sell tyres made by a German company. It had 25,000 shares issued, only one of which was held by a non-German national and all of its directors were German. During the First World War against Germany the appellant company, Daimler Ltd, claimed that it did not have to pay money it owed to the respondent company since to do so would constitute 'trading with the enemy'.

Held The House of Lords reiterated the basic proposition that the identity of a company's shareholders was immaterial to the company's separate legal personality. However, they allowed for the possibility that there will be occasions when the shareholders' identity does affect the law's view of corporate personality, such as in time of war as in the present case. The enemy character of the persons in *de facto* control of the company imparted itself to the company so that the company could be said to be under the control of the enemy. The appeal was therefore allowed.

1.2.4   Agency

Re FG (Films) Ltd (1953)

FG (Films) Ltd had applied under the then relevant legislation to have a film declared 'British'. The application was refused on the ground that the film had really been made by a large US film company, FG Incorporated. This US company had agreed to provide FG (Films) Ltd with finance and all necessary facilities to make the film. FG (Films) Ltd had a registered office in the UK but no actual place of business in the UK, and it employed no staff in the UK. Ninety per cent of its shares were owned by a US national director with the remaining 10% owned by a UK national director. It sought a declaration from the court that it was the 'maker' of the film in question and, since it was a UK registered company, then the film was British.

Held The court did not grant the declaration sought. Instead it held that the UK company was merely the agent of the US company and in no sense the true maker of the film. the evidence showed that it had been brought into existence as a mere corporate shell in an attempt to qualify the film as British. The court said it was contrary to both fact and reason to say that this insignificant company had in any sense undertaken the making of the film.

Trebanog Working Men's Club v Macdonald (1940)

The club was incorporated as a company under the Industrial and Provident Societies legislation. The company was charged with contravention of the licensing laws in that it was selling liquor to its members without a licence.

Held The company had not sold liquor to its members without a licence. The court conducted a legal analysis of what was going on when a member 'bought' a drink at the club bar. The court held it was not a straightforward contract of sale with the member buying the company's property. Instead, they characterised the company as a trustee of the liquor, holding it under trust according to the club rules for the members beneficially so the transaction at the club bar was a transfer of a special property in the liquor from all the members of the club to the one member buying the drink. This is an obvious exception to the *Macaura* case considered above, 1.1

1.2.5 Statutory lifting of the veil

Re Produce Marketing Consortium Ltd (No 2) (1989)
Considered in Part 4.

British Airways Board v Parish (1979)
The defendant had inadvertently omitted the word 'limited' from the company's name when he signed a company cheque. The payee of the cheque agreed payment by instalments with the company of the amount due under the cheque.

Held The director was still nevertheless personally liable under what is now s 349(4) of the Companies Act 1985.

2 Acts of the company

2.1 Commission of crimes and torts by the company

2.1.1 *Mens rea* of the company

Lennard's Carrying Co Ltd v Asiatic Petroleum Co Ltd (1915) HL

The appellants were ship owners and one of their ships caught fire due to its unseaworthy condition, destroying its cargo. When sued by the cargo owners the appellants relied on the statutory let out in the Merchant Shipping Act 1894 that they would not be liable for damages to cargo owners where the loss occurred without their 'actual fault or privity'. The managing director of the appellant company was in full control of the management of the ship.

Held Because of the position he enjoyed, the acts of the managing director in managing the ship could be seen as the acts of the company. The appellant company was responsible for his acts and defaults and so the company could not escape liability by relying on the statutory defence.

Tesco Supermarkets Ltd v Nattrass (1972) HL

The appellant company was charged with an offence under the trade descriptions legislation of displaying inaccurate price information in one of its stores. The company was convicted and fined but appealed on the basis that the company had not committed the offence – it had in place a management and supervisory system designed to prevent this type of offence and the failure that resulted in the offence being committed was the failure of the store supervisor, which should not be attributed to the company.

Held The appeal succeeded. Because the store supervisory manager could not be said to be part of the 'directing mind and will' of the company his acts could not be said to be those of the company. The House of Lords stressed the fictional nature of the corporate legal person and the need to distinguish between:

- acts which were actually those of the company; and
- acts which were those of an agent or servant of the company but for which the company has some statutory or vicarious liability.

The former category are usually those acts committed by the board of directors or senior management of a company who speak and act for it. They are its 'brain' or its 'nerve centre'.

Director General of Fair Trading v Pioneer Concrete (UK) Ltd and another (In Re supply of ready mixed concrete (No 2)) (1995) HL

The respondent companies had, at a senior level, promulgated and put in place compliance systems to ensure that no employee breached injunctions restraining contravention of restrictive trade practices legislation. However, contrary to the companies' express instructions and without their knowledge, some of the employees went ahead and ignored the injunctions. The companies argued that they should not be vicariously liable for the acts of these employees as they acted without any form of authority and contrary to explicit instructions. The court at first instance disagreed and held the companies to be nonetheless in contempt of court. The Court of Appeal allowed the companies' appeal and the Director General of Fair Trading, who is responsible for the enforcement of restrictive practices legislation, appealed to the House of Lords.

Held The appeal was allowed. Since a company is a fictional person it can only act through the medium of its agents and the actions of its employees acting in the course of their employment amount to the carrying on of business by the company. Simply because a prohibition at senior level existed, designed to prevent illegal agreements being made, was not enough to prevent the companies becoming party to such agreements where the prohibition was ignored by the employees. Lord Templeman said that '... an employee who acts for the company within the scope of his employment is the company. Directors may give instructions, top management may exhort, middle management may question and workers may listen attentively. But if a worker makes a defective product or a lower manager accepts or rejects an order, he is the company'.

Meridian Global Funds Management Asia Ltd v Securities Commission (1995) PC

This case concerned an attempt by predators based in New Zealand, Malaysia and Hong Kong to gain control of, and strip assets and cash from, a publicly listed New Zealand company ('ENC'). The predators included a New Zealand businessman, a Malaysian stockbroking firm and two gentleman referred to throughout the case as 'Koo' and 'Ng'. Koo and Ng were employed by the appellant company, Meridian Global Funds Management Asia Ltd ('Meridian') and were, respectively, its chief investment officer and a senior portfolio manager. The appellant company was a Hong Kong investment management company with an Australian parent company, and although Koo was at the relevant time under the appellant's managing director in the corporate hierarchy of Meridian, in practice the evidence showed that he was given a very free rein in the conduct of the business of the company. The group of predators intended to ultimately finance their purchase of a controlling interest in ENC by using its own assets but interim finance was needed in order to buy the shares which would give them control of ENC's monies and assets. This was provided by Koo and Ng out of funds managed by Meridian as they improperly used their authority to act on behalf of Meridian and bought and re-sold shares in various Asian companies. However, the plan misfired at the final stage when independent directors of ENC frustrated the predators' use of ENC's funds to repay Meridian. The result was that Meridian's Australian parent had to make good the losses suffered by the managed funds' beneficial owners. The New Zealand Securities Commission brought an action in the High Court of New Zealand, against Meridian for failure to disclose the fact that it had become a substantial holder of securities in a public company. Meridian argued that it did not have the requisite knowledge but the High Court attributed to Meridian the knowledge of Koo and Ng of the fact that Meridian was a substantial security holder. The New Zealand Court of Appeal affirmed this decision, attributing Koo's knowledge to Meridian on the ground that he was 'the directing mind and will' of the company. Meridian appealed to the Privy Council.

Held Meridian's appeal failed. However in dismissing the appeal Lord Hoffmann, giving the judgment of the Privy Council, did not apply the same legal basis for attribution to Meridian of knowledge of the extent of its interest as was used by the Court of Appeal. Having analysed both the *Tesco Supermarkets v Natrass* and *In Re supply of ready mixed concrete (No 2)* decisions of the House of Lords, he concluded that neither case provides an appropriate basis or general formula of attribution which will fit all the widely varying situations in which companies may or may not be responsible in law for the acts of those purportedly acting on their behalf. Instead, the task becomes one of examination of the context, content and policy of the particular legal obligation or rule in question. Put like this, the question of whether or not Koo's knowledge could be attributed to Meridian answers itself most obviously – it has to be in order for the disclosure provisions of New Zealand securities legislation to be at all meaningful. Hence, Meridian's appeal was dismissed and the declaration that Meridian was in breach of its duty to notify the Securities Commission that it had become a substantial holder of securities in a public company.

2.1.2   The company as perpetrator of dishonesty offences

DPP v Kent and Sussex Contractors Ltd (1944)
The company was charged with making use of false documentation with intent to deceive and making a statement known to be false in a material particular, which constituted offences under fuel rationing regulations in force at the time. It was the company's transport manager who had *de facto* done the acts in question in the course of his employment and on behalf of the company. The question arose as to whether a company could be said to form the requisite 'guilty' intention or have the appropriate 'knowledge'

of falsehood for these offences to be constituted by virtue of the fact that one of its agents had such intent and knowledge.

Held The company was capable of having knowledge and forming an intent to do an act and so was capable of being guilty of the offences charged. The company had, through the medium of the only people who were capable of acting, speaking or thinking for it (namely the transport manager – and the court said the officers of the company were the company for this purpose), formed the requisite intention to deceive and made a false statement. The Divisional Court acknowledged that a company could not be guilty of treason or a criminal offence for which the only punishment was death or imprisonment.

R v JCR Haulage Ltd (1944) CA

This was an appeal by the company against a conviction, along with other co-conspirators including its managing director, for the common law offence of conspiracy to defraud. It was contended on behalf of the company that, since dishonesty was an essential ingredient of this offence, the company could not be guilty since a company, lacking a mind, could not be said to honest or dishonest.

Held The appeal was disallowed. The Court of Appeal, while accepting that there were some offences such as perjury, bigamy and capital offences which a company could not logically be capable of committing, agreed with the prosecution's case that just as certain acts could be attributed from the human agents of a company to that company so too could an intention or state of mind. Consequently, the fraud of the managing director in this case could be said to be the fraud of the company.

R v McDonnell (1966)

The defendant, McDonnell, was the sole controller with complete authority to act for two companies. He was charged and convicted of conspiracy to defraud with these two companies. He appealed his conviction on the grounds that his mind was for all intents and purposes the mind of both of these companies so that there was in reality only one controlling mind and a conspiracy required the agreement of at least two minds.

Held His appeal succeeded. Since the defendant was proved to have acted alone as far as these two companies were concerned and although the companies were certainly separate legal entities they should not be regarded as separate minds or persons for the purposes of a conspiracy charge.

2.1.3 The company as victim of dishonesty offences

Attorney General's Reference (No 2 of 1982) (1984) CA

The defendants had been charged with theft from companies of which they were sole directors and shareholders. They had been acquitted since the jury had been directed that, following *Tesco Supermarkets v Nattrass*, the sole owners of a company were its directing mind and will and therefore could not be said to steal from it. This point of law was referred to the Court of Appeal.

Held The judge's interpretation of *Tesco Supermarkets* was wrong – that case's reasoning related to the company as perpetrator not victim of offences. Where all the members/directors, even if they are sole controllers of a company, act illegally and dishonestly appropriate that company's property they can be said to be guilty of theft.

R v Philippou (1989) CA

The two directors were the sole directors and shareholders of a group of holiday companies. The three principal companies in the group went into liquidation in 1984. During the year prior to the liquidation, the directors bought a block of flats in Spain which had been used by one of these three companies. They used this company's money to fund the purchase and then transferred the block of flats to a Spanish company of which they were the only shareholders. The two directors appealed from their conviction for theft from the company on the grounds that they were the 'mind and will' of the company since they were the only members and directors and therefore the company had instructed the bank to use its own money to fund the flats purchase so it had consented to the payment.

Held The appeal was disallowed. The instruction from the company to its bankers to pay for the flats was but one element in a series of transactions which enriched the defendants personally. It was quite possible in law for sole directors and shareholders to steal from their company.

R v Rozeik (1996) CA

The defendant had been convicted of dishonestly obtaining by deception cheques from finance companies contrary to s 15 of the Theft Act 1968. He had allegedly furnished the finance companies with false information and invoices as the basis of his dishonest applications for funds. It was accepted by the prosecution that the branch managers of the finance companies may not have been deceived and were probably aware of the falsity of the representations made by the defendant. However, no evidence was adduced to show that these branch managers were acting dishonestly or were a party to the fraud being practiced by the defendant. The trial judge's directions to the jury on the question of whether or not the companies were deceived contained a direction to assume that the branch managers knew that the invoices were false and therefore to ignore the effect of their state of mind. He further directed that, the branch managers aside, if any other employee or employees within the companies were deceived by the false invoices into doing something which resulted in cheques being obtained by the defendant, then that was sufficient to find him guilty of obtaining by deception as against the companies.

The defendant appealed against his conviction for theft on the grounds that the judge had misdirected the jury in so far as he was wrong to decide that persons within a company other than those responsible for making decisions to authorise the respective transactions were persons who could be deceived and whose deception could be attributed to the company. He also argued that the branch managers' knowledge of the deception should be imputed to the companies which, therefore, could not be said to have been deceived for the purposes of s 15 of the Theft Act 1968.

Held The Court of Appeal allowed the appeal. Lord Justice Leggatt said:

> ... where one employee is deceived by a representation but either the true position or the falsity of the representation is known to another employee (or at least to another employee in a position of equality or superiority to the employee deceived) the company cannot be said to have been deceived ... The offence is committed against the company, and not the individual employee, so if the company is fixed with knowledge of the true position it is not deceived.

Lord Justice Leggatt assessed this contention in the light of the decision in *Meridian Global Funds Management v Securities Commission* and *In Re supply of ready mixed concrete (No 2)* decisions concerning the attribution of acts and knowledge of its employees to a company in order to fix it with liability as a perpetrator. He said that, for the purpose of ascertaining whose state of mind represented the state of mind of the company as to whether it had been deceived into entering into the hire-purchase agreements, it was the branch managers (who had the entire conduct of these transactions) who were the relevant people. Since they were not proved to have been acting dishonestly then their knowledge that the invoices were false should be attributed to the company.

2.1.4 Companies and torts

Campbell v Paddington Corporation (1911)

The plaintiff let premises for the viewing of a royal funeral procession. However the view was obscured by the unlawful erection of a stand by the defendant corporation. She sued it for damages in tort.

Held The corporation was liable for losses caused by the unlawful act which its council had resolved to do. The resolution to do the act was the resolution of the corporation and therefore the act was the act of the corporation.

2.2 *Ultra vires* acts by the company

2.2.1 When is an act *ultra vires* the company's memorandum?

Ashbury Railway Carriage & Iron Co Ltd v Riche (1875) HL

The objects clause in the appellant company's memorandum of association empowered the company to make railway carriages and rolling stock, to carry on business as mechanical engineers, and to trade in timber, coal, metals etc. The company's memorandum then went on to state 'An extension of the company's business beyond or for other than the objects or purposes expressed or implied in the memorandum of association shall take place only in pursuance of a special resolution'. The company entered into an agreement with the respondent to finance a railway construction project. When it subsequently repudiated this agreement and was sued for damages it relied on the argument that the agreement was void and ineffective for being *ultra vires* its powers.

Held Whether or not any ratification by special resolution had taken place was immaterial, the agreement was *ultra vires* and therefore void. Lord Cairns LC emphasised that the memorandum states the outer limits of what constitutes a company's 'vitality and power'. It cannot exceed those limits. Even if all the shareholders unanimously consent it makes no difference, if a contract is beyond the competence and power of a company then it is void *ab initio* and nothing the members subsequently do can save it.

Re German Date Coffee (1882) CA

A company was incorporated with its stated objects being to acquire and exploit a German patent for a process of manufacturing coffee from dates. It failed to do acquire the patent from the German authorities but nevertheless had established manufacturing facilities in Germany and was doing a prosperous trade in the coffee substitute. Two shareholders objected to the company carrying on business and applied to wind the company up.

Held The winding up petition was granted. The Court of Appeal said that the underlying purpose for which the company had been set up had not been achieved. Its interpretation of the company's objects clause in its memorandum was that the company's business was to acquire and exploit the German patent, not to carry on this unauthorised manufacturing business. Its objects had failed and the business it was now carrying on was *ultra vires*.

2.2.2 The construction of objects clauses

Cotman v Brougham (1918) HL

The objects clause of a company enabled it to carry on nearly every type of commercial activity under the sun and was exhaustively drafted in minute detail. The final sub-clause expressly stated that each sub-clause should be construed as a self-contained substantive object of the company with none of them being ancillary or subsidiary to the principal object of the company. A dispute arose as to whether or not the company was authorised to underwrite a share issue in another company.

Held The objects clause of the memorandum was so widely drafted that the transaction was in fact *intra vires*. The House of Lords expressed unhappiness at the prevalence of this type of blanket and indiscriminate drafting of objects clauses but said the express wording of the memorandum meant that there was no basis upon which they could cut down the company's powers. They suggested any remedy of what they termed the abuses of this type of drafting was the job of Parliament.

Bell Houses Ltd v City Wall Properties Ltd (1966) CA

The plaintiff company carried on business as property developers. In return for a promise from the defendant company to pay an introducer's fee the plaintiff put them in touch with a financier. The fee was not paid and when they sued for it they were met with the argument from the defendant that they were not entitled to it as mortgage broking was *ultra vires* the plaintiff's business. The plaintiff's objects clause contained a phrase permitting them 'to carry on any other trade or business whatsoever which can, in the opinion of the board of directors, be advantageously carried on by the company in connection with or as ancillary to any of the above businesses or the general business of the company'. The plaintiff company appealed to the Court of Appeal relying on this sub-clause to argue that their financial broking activities were *intra vires*.

Held The appeal succeeded. The plain and natural meaning of the sub-clause was such as to render this ancillary business *intra vires*.

Re Introductions Ltd (1970) CA

This company was incorporated in 1951 and began trading offering hospitality services, then deck chair rental, then, after a two year hiatus, ventured into pig breeding in 1960. This venture proved disastrous and it went into liquidation in 1965 after having borrowed extensively from the bank. When the bank tried to enforce the security it had been granted it was met by argument from the liquidator that it was unenforceable as the company's borrowing had been *ultra vires* the company's objects and so the security granted was void. The company's memorandum contained an objects clause in similar terms to that used in *Cotman v Brougham* with one of the sub-clauses conferring a power to borrow but there was no sub-clause conferring authority to breed pigs. The bank knew of the purpose of the loan.

Held The breeding of pigs was clearly *ultra vires* and the bank had notice of that. The bank could not argue that the company's borrowing for the purposes of an *ultra vires* object (pig breeding) was in itself an *intra vires* object. Borrowing is an incidental power and not a self-standing substantive object;

the express wording of the memorandum did not elevate something into an object which was not capable of being an object.

Re Horsley & Weight Ltd (1982) CA

The company's memorandum included a clause giving the company power to grant pensions to employees and ex-employees. It also stated that each object was to be construed as a separate and distinct object. The company took out a pension policy for a retiring director which was impugned a year later by the liquidator as being *ultra vires* and therefore void.

Held There is nothing to prevent a company having charitable or philanthropic objects as well as commercial ones. In this case, the gratuitous payment was within the declared objects of the company and therefore not *ultra vires*.

2.2.3   The doctrine of constructive notice and the *ultra vires* rule

Re David Payne & Co Ltd (1904) CA

The company was empowered by its memorandum to borrow money and grant security for the purposes of its business. It borrowed money, secured by a debenture, from a mineral exploration company. The money had in fact been borrowed for a purpose that was *ultra vires* David Payne & Co Ltd's objects but the lender did not know the purpose of the loan. The liquidator resisted enforcement of the debenture security on the grounds that the borrowing was void.

Held The debenture was valid. The lender did not know the purpose of the loan and was therefore entitled to assume that it was for *intra vires* activities of the company. Where a company's memorandum empowered the company to borrow for the purposes of its business the onus was not on any lender to enquire as to whether the purposes for which lawful borrowing was sought were in fact within the scope of the company's objects.

Re Jon Beauforte (London) Ltd (1953)

This case concerned an action to recover contract debts brought by a firm of coke suppliers against the liquidator of Jon Beauforte (London) Ltd. The company had been formed with the main object of dress and costume making but also had the type of 'ancillary objects' clause considered in *Bell Houses* (above). The company decided to branch out and diversify into the manufacture of veneered panels, which was an *ultra vires* purpose. The coke suppliers had contracted with the company knowing that it was holding itself out as a veneered panel manufacturer and required the coke for use for this purpose.

Held The coke suppliers could not claim the contract price they were owed as they had constructive notice of the memorandum of Jon Beauforte (London) Ltd by virtue of its public registration, and therefore ought to have appreciated that the purposes for which the coke was ordered (of which they also had clear notice) were *ultra vires*.

2.2.4 Directors doing *intra vires* act for improper purpose

Rolled Steel Products (Holdings) Ltd v British Steel Corporation and others (1986) CA

The appellant company's memorandum empowered it to give guarantees. It guaranteed obligations owed by one of its associated companies to the respondent company. The giving of these guarantees was not for the benefit of its business at all but was to the personal advantage of one of the appellant company's directors. Thus, it was an improper use of this power under the memorandum by the directors. The court at first instance thought that this abuse of power by the directors rendered the guarantees unenforceable and void for being *ultra vires* the company's objects.

Held The fact that what was done was done out of improper motives on the part of the directors did not alter the fact that the company was in law capable of doing it. It had the capacity to give these guarantees and the reasons for which the directors caused the company to exercise that capacity could not be significant so as to convert an otherwise perfectly lawful act by the company into an *ultra vires* one.

2.3 Unauthorised acts by the company's officers

See 5.4.2 on directors' authority to bind the company.

3 Formation of the company

3.1 The company's name

Ewing v Buttercup Margarine Co Ltd (1917) CA

The plaintiff operated a retail business known as 'The Buttercup Dairy Company'. The defendant company wished to trade as wholesalers of margarine. It would not sell its product direct to the public. The plaintiff sought to restrain the defendant company from continuing to trade under its present name on the grounds that the use of the name may induce the belief that the defendant's goods are actually those of the plaintiff or that the defendant company's business is an extension of, or in some way connected to, the plaintiff's business.

Held The plaintiff was granted the relief sought.

Exxon Corporation v Exxon Insurance Consultants International Ltd (1982)

The defendant company carried on business as motor insurance brokers and were in no way connected with the plaintiff company who were an international oil company with a global presence identified with the name 'Exxon'. The plaintiff company sought an injunction preventing the use of the word Exxon in the defendant company's name.

Held The protection of the common law tort of passing off extended to cover this case and prevent the defendant from using the name 'Exxon' even though the defendant was not in the same line of business as the plaintiff, since the public might still be likely to do business with the defendant company as the name 'Exxon' is so widely known that it may lead to an erroneous impression that a connection exists where there is in fact none.

3.2 Registration

Bowman v Secular Society Ltd (1917) HL

The defendant company was registered under the Companies Acts with its principal object being the promotion of secularism. The plaintiff alleged that this was contrary to public policy.

Held The House of Lords did not in fact consider this an unlawful object but they did go on to pronounce more generally on the effect of the issuance of a certificate of incorporation. The effect of the certificate of incorporation is not such so as to confer legality on illegal objects but the general public does not have standing to go behind the certificate of incorporation and challenge the status of a duly incorporated company. Only the Attorney General has such standing.

R v Registrar of Companies, ex p Attorney General (1991)

Ms Lindi St Clair set up a company through which to carry out her trade as a prostitute. She had applied for registration of this company under the names 'Prostitutes Ltd', 'Hookers Ltd', and 'Lindi St Clair (French Lessons) Ltd' all of which were rejected by the Registrar of Companies. Eventually the company was registered with the name 'Lindi St Clair (Personal Services) Ltd'. The Attorney General brought an action to challenge the registration of the company on the grounds that its purposes were unlawful.

Held The company was struck off the register as its principal objects were illegal, contracts being made for sexually immoral purposes being contrary to public policy and illegal.

3.3 Duties of promoters

Twycross v Grant (1877)

The plaintiff sued the defendants in damages for breach of the statutory prospectus disclosure requirements then in force.

Held The defendants were liable for damages. Cockburn CJ opined on what constitutes a promoter: 'A promoter ... is one who undertakes to form a company with reference to a given project and to set it going, and who takes the necessary steps to accomplish that purpose.' As to when one ceases to be a promoter, that is always a question of fact and is not necessarily the same time as when the board of directors are appointed. The functions of a promoter *vis à vis* the formation of a company may in fact continue for some time after the company's directors have taken up the reins of governance.

Emma Silver Mining Co v Lewis (1879) CPD

The defendants in this case were metal brokers who assisted Mr Park to sell a silver mine at a grossly inflated value to the plaintiff company. They assisted Park in its flotation, featured in the prospectus and failed to disclose information pertinent to the true value of the mine. In turn they received commission and generous remuneration. When subsequently sued by the plaintiff company for damages they argued they were not promoters of the company as such.

Held The defendants were indeed capable of being held to be promoters. Since this is a question of fact it was referred to the jury by a the trial judge who answered in the affirmative. Lindley J repeated the finding in *Twycross v Grant*, that the term 'promoter' was not a term of art. It connotes someone who, firstly, exerts himself for the purpose of floating a company and, secondly, has imposed on him some sort of duty to the company by virtue of the position he has assumed towards it. Even after incorporation the company's directors are by no means the only persons who may owe it fiduciary duties.

Erlanger v New Sombrero Phosphate Co (1878) HL

The appellant, Erlanger, formed a business syndicate which bought for £55,000 the lease of an island and its phosphate extraction rights. The respondent company was then formed by the syndicate. Of its first directors, only one was independent of the syndicate, the remainder being controlled by Erlanger. The island lease was then sold via a nominee to the respondent company for £110,000. A few days after incorporation the respondent company's directors met and ratified the acquisition. Shares in the company were then sold to investors to whom no disclosure was ever made about the sale and purchase of the island. The truth was discovered a few months later and the shareholders appointed a new board of directors. The company now applied to have the sale of the island lease rescinded.

Held Erlanger's syndicate were promoters of the company and stood in a fiduciary position with respect to it, owing it fiduciary duties. Unless full and frank disclosure was made to an independent board of the company about all material facts relating to a transaction between promoters and the company, then that transaction was voidable at the instance of the company. Lord Cairns LC said:

> I do not say that the owner of ... property may not promote and form a joint stock company, and then sell his property to it, but I do say that if he does he is bound to take care that he sells it to the company through the medium of a board of directors who can and do exercise an independent and intelligent judgment on the transaction, and who are not left under the belief that the property belongs, not to the promoter, but to some other person ...

Gluckstein v Barnes (1900) HL

The appellant, Gluckstein, acting with three associates jointly purchased premises for £140,000. They then re-sold them for £180,000 to a company they formed and promoted especially for this purpose. They also bought securities on the property which they subsequently enforced at a personal profit to them of £20,000. The company had no independent directors and its prospectus inviting subscription disclosed the £40,000 profit on the premises sale but not the £20,000 profit on the securities transactions. The company went into liquidation and the liquidator claimed Gluckstein's share of the £20,000.

Held The House of Lords unanimously agreed with the lower courts' finding that Gluckstein was liable to account to the company for the amount sought. Lord Halsbury LC said full disclosure should have been made to the company. It was not sufficient disclosure that the directors of the company (who were in fact Gluckstein and his associates) knew of the details of the transaction and hence the secret profit made by the promoters. For they were the very people who were practising what was described as very gross fraud on the shareholders.

Lagunas Nitrate Company v Lagunas Syndicate (1899) CA

The directors of the Lagunas Nitrate Syndicate formed the appellant company, the Lagunas Nitrate Company, to buy property belonging to the syndicate company, which was seen in law as responsible for the acts and omissions of its directors and hence was seen as promoter of the appellant company. The two companies duly executed an agreement to sell the property. The appellant company attempted to have the agreement rescinded relying (*inter alia*) on the *Erlanger v New Sombreo Phosphate Co* decision and arguing that the formation of the appellant company was improper as the promoters had failed to provide it with an independent board of directors.

Held This in itself, and in the absence of fraud or concealment by the promoters, was not enough to allow rescission. It is not the duty of promoters of a company to provide it with an independent board of directors.

Re Cape Breton Company (1887) HL

A company bought coal fields from a business syndicate. One of its directors was an undisclosed member of that syndicate. The company paid considerably more for the property than did the syndicate. The syndicate had bought the coal fields two years before it sold them to the company; two more years elapsed then the company went into liquidation; three years later the members of the company voted to affirm the original purchase and the liquidator sold the coal fields off at a loss.

Held The company, having affirmed the contract, could not hold the director/syndicate member accountable for his original profit.

Whaley Bridge Calico Printing Co v Green (1880) 5 QBD 109

Bowen J said: 'The term promoter is a term not of law, but of business, usefully summing up in a single word a number of business operations familiar to the commercial world by which a company is generally brought into existence.' He also ruled that a company may enforce the personal claims of a promoter against a party who has undertaken to pay the promoter a profit, bribe or other benefit in connection with the promotion. This is because the law sees the promoter as analogous to a trustee of his claim for the company's benefit.

3.4   Pre-incorporation contracts

3.4.1   The position at common law

Natal Land & Colonisation Co Ltd v Pauline Colliery & Development Syndicate Ltd (1904) PC

This action was brought by the respondent company for specific performance of an agreement to lease mining rights from the appellant company. The respondent company was not incorporated until January 1898 yet the agreement was entered into in December 1897 ostensibly between the appellant company's agent and an individual acting on behalf of the unincorporated business syndicate which was forming and promoting the respondent company.

Held There was no contract in existence between the two companies. A company cannot, by adoption or ratification, obtain the benefit of a contract ostensibly made on its behalf before it even came into existence as a legal person.

Kelner v Baxter (1866)

Mr Kelner agreed with the promoters of an unformed company to sell wine to the company. The promoters purported to act 'on behalf of the company' even though it was, at the time of contracting, unformed. The promoters took delivery of the wine. After incorporation the company failed before Kelner had been paid so he sued the promoters personally for the contract price.

Held The promoters were personally liable on the contract. Although the promoters concluded the agreement as agents there was no principal in existence so there could be no agency. Hence the promoters were themselves bound by the contract.

Newborne v Sensolid (Great Britain) Ltd (1954) CA

Mr Newborne, the plaintiff, signed a letter confirming an agreement to sell ham to the defendant. He signed it purportedly on behalf of a company which did not at that time exist. He then attempted to enforce the agreement in his personal capacity relying on the fact that he had signed on behalf of an unformed company, would, following *Kelner v Baxter*, be personally liable on the agreement and therefore ought to be able to enforce it personally.

Held There was no personal right of action on this contract. Indeed, there was no contract as one of the parties (the company) did not exist. The contract purported to be for the company's benefit not Mr Newborne's and just because the company did not in fact exist when the contract was made did not mean the benefit of the contract was then conferred on Mr Newborne.

3.4.2 The position subsequent to s 36C of the Companies Act 1985

Phonogram Ltd v Lane (1982) CA

It was planned to form a new company to manage a rock band. Financial negotiations were taking place prior to its formation between Phonogram Ltd and Mr Lane. Mr Lane agreed a loan 'for and on behalf of' the as yet unformed company. In fact, it never was formed and an action was brought against Mr Lane for repayment of the monies which had been advanced to the rock band pursuant to the loan agreement.

Held Lane was personally liable to repay the loan. Lord Denning MR made it clear in his judgment that the new s 36C dispensed with all the pre-existing fine distinctions of agency drawn by the old case law on this issue. He said that unless there is a clear exclusion of personal liability, s 36C should be given its full and literal effect so that in all cases such as this where a person purports to contract on behalf of a company not yet formed, then, however he expresses his signature, in the absence of clear contrary agreement he is personally liable on that contract.

Oshkosh B'Gosh Inc v Dan Marbel Inc Ltd (1989)

Mr C bought a ready formed company off the shelf and changed its name. Before the name change took effect the company purchased goods, acting through the medium of Mr C, from the plaintiff. The plaintiff now sought to make Mr C personally liable on this purchase contract relying on s 9(2) of the European Communities Act 1972 (the predecessor of s 36C).

Held The action failed, the statutory provision being inapplicable in the instance where the company was already incorporated but merely changing its name. Its existence and legal personality at the time of the contract was not in doubt.

Cotronic (UK) Ltd v Dezonie (1991) CA

The respondent, Dezonie signed a contract in 1986 on behalf of a company, WB Ltd with the appellant, Cotronic Ltd. He believed WB Ltd to be in existence but in fact it had been struck off the Companies Register as defunct under s 652 in 1981. When Dezonie discovered this in 1989 he formed a new company WB Ltd and then tried to rely on s 36C to personally claim the benefit of the contract with the (then) non-existent company.

Held (Without resolving the issue of whether or not s 36C may be used to enforce a contract personally – that question is still open.) Because Dezonie believed in 1986 that the original WB Ltd was still in existence he could not turn round at a later date and argue that he made the contract on behalf of the second WB Ltd (formed in 1989). He never even envisaged the existence of this second company in 1986 at the date of contracting, hence it was not a situation to which s 36C was applicable.

3.5 Prospectuses and listing particulars

3.5.1 Contractual misrepresentation

Coles v White City (Manchester) Greyhound Association Ltd (1928)
The defendant company's prospectus claimed that property it owned was suitable for the purposes of greyhound racing but omitted to state that this was subject to the company obtaining local authority planning consent for viewing stands and kennels.

Held A shareholder was entitled to rescission of his contract to subscribe for shares in the company on the basis of the misleading omission.

Sharpley v Louth and East Coast Railway Company (1876) 2 Ch D 663
Held The shareholder was barred from obtaining rescission since he had, subsequent to discovering the original misrepresentation, accepted it in the sense that he had exercised his rights of membership by voting at a meeting. This affirmed the contract and negated the misrepresentation.

3.5.2 Tort of deceit

Derry v Peek (1889) HL
The appellants were directors of a company which issued a prospectus claiming that it had an absolute statutory right to run steam and mechanically powered trams. In fact, no such absolute statutory right existed but was dependent upon government consents which were not subsequently forthcoming. Upon the company being wound up, the respondent brought an action in the tort of deceit for damages against the appellants based on the fraudulent misrepresentations contained in the prospectus which he asserted induced him to subscribe for shares in the company.

Held The appeal succeeded as the House of Lords thought that the respondents had been careless rather than fraudulent and proof nothing short of fraud is necessary to sustain an action in deceit. They did, however, point to the urgent need for legislative intervention, preferably in the form of a right of action for breach of statutory duty, to ensure some protection for those investing in companies on the strength of prospectuses containing information which is not strictly verified and statements that are carelessly made.

3.5.3 Negligent misstatements

Hedley Byrne & Co Ltd v Heller & Partners Ltd (1964) HL
Held Provided there is a sufficiently proximate relationship so that a duty of care is owed then an action for damages will lie for a negligent misstatement which is relied on in such a way that it causes economic loss.

Caparo Industries plc v Dickman & others (1990) HL

The defendants had audited the accounts of Fidelity plc. The plaintiffs, Caparo plc, were shareholders in Fidelity plc and made a successful takeover bid, acquiring all its shares. The accounts showed a profit of £1.2 million whereas in reality there had been a loss of £0.4 million. The plaintiffs thought they had paid too much for Fidelity shares and they blamed this on the erroneous accounts which they claimed caused the shares to be overvalued and were, they alleged, the result of the defendant's negligence. They sued in damages for negligent misstatement basing their claim on the *Hedley Byrne* principle.

Held Conscious of the dangers of opening the floodgates of litigation to claims against auditors the House of Lords rejected the claim, ruling that the defendants were not under a duty of care to the plaintiffs. They said auditors of a public company's accounts owe no duty of care to members of the public at large who rely upon the accounts in deciding whether to buy shares in the company.

Al-Nakib Investments (Jersey) Ltd v Longcroft (1990)

The plaintiff, Al-Nakib, subscribed for shares in M Ltd and bought shares already in issue on the USM. The prospectus for M Ltd claimed that a computer system was operational and ready to market when in fact it was not. The plaintiff sued the defendants, directors of M Ltd, in damages on the basis of the untrue statements in the prospectus.

Held An action in damages would not lie in respect of the USM market purchases but only in respect of the subscription for new shares. This was because statements in a prospectus were made for a particular purpose – informing the basis of an investor's decision to subscribe or not to subscribe for new shares. Hence, no duty of care is owed when the prospectus is in fact used for an entirely different purpose – purchase of existing shares on the secondary markets – as that is not a purpose for which a prospectus is issued and statements therein are made.

Possfund Custodian Trustee Ltd v Diamond (1996)

D plc issued a prospectus relating to its shares which were being floated on the unlisted securities market ('USM'). The prospectus contained a statement that as part of the allotment exercise a dealing facility would be made available so that the shares could be sold on the USM subsequent to their allotment. Most of the plaintiffs in this action were original subscribers to the shares but some had bought shares on the USM subsequent to their being allotted (these were referred to in the judgment as 'after market purchasers'). The plaintiffs brought an action against D plc, its directors, auditors and advisers claiming damages for deceit and/or negligent misstatement in connection with statements made in the prospectus. The defendants applied to have the claims of the after market purchasers struck out on the grounds that no common law duty of care was owed to these subsequent purchasers following *Caparo* and *Al-Nakib*.

Held Mr Justice Lightman refused to strike out the plaintiffs' claims. He said there was an arguable issue here provided that the subsequent purchaser could prove that he bought the shares in reliance on a prospectus statement, and that he reasonably believed the maker of the statement intended him to do so. There might exist circumstances where, despite the decisions in *Caparo* and *Al-Nakib*, it was fair and reasonable to hold that a duty of care was owed by the respresentor to a subsequent purchaser, if, for example, the plaintiffs could show that the original prospectus was prepared and circulated with the intention of encouraging after market purchases, then prospectus duties could be owed beyond the original immediate purchasers. The claims of the after market purchasers were therefore allowed to proceed.

4 Articles of association

4.1 The legal effect of articles of association

4.1.1 Memorandum takes precedence over articles

Guinness v Land Corporation of Ireland (1882) CA
The objects of the company as stated in the memorandum were land culti-vation. The capital clause of the memorandum stated that the capital was divided into Class A shares and Class B shares. The articles of association provided that, if necessary, capital from the Class B shares should be applied in the payment of a 5% dividend on the Class A shares. One of the Class B shareholders applied to the court for a ruling on the effect of this provision in the articles.

Held The provision in the articles was invalid. Bowen LJ said:

> It seems to me that the collocation of the two things, the compulsory statement of the objects of the company in the first place, and the compulsory statement of the capital in the second place, produces at once the legal obligation that the company shall devote to those objects alone the capital which is subscribed, and I think that the other sections of the Act are based upon the assumption that this is so.

4.1.2 Effect of the section 14 contract

Wood v Odessa Waterworks Company (1889)
The articles of association provided that the directors could, with the sanc-tion of the members in general meeting, declare a dividend to be paid to the members in proportion to their shares. An ordinary resolution was passed approving a proposal from the directors that dividends be paid not in cash but instead by way of a distribution of debentures to shareholders. A minority shareholder applied to court for an injunction to restrain the company from paying the dividend in this way.

Held The injunction was granted as the proposed payment was incon-sistent with the provisions of the articles of association and the minority shareholder was entitled to enforce said articles.

Stirling J said:

> ... [T]he rights of shareholders in respect of a division of the profits of the company are governed by the provisions in the articles of association. By s 16 of

the Companies Act 1862 [s 14 of the CA 1985] the articles of association 'bind the company and its members thereof to the same extent as if each member had subscribed his name and affixed his seal thereto, and there were in such articles contained a covenant on the part of himself ... to conform to all the regulations contained in such articles, subject to the provisions of this Act.' [Section 9 of the CA 1985] provides for means for altering the regulations of the company contained in the articles of association by passing a special resolution, but no such resolution has in this case been passed or attempted to be passed; and the question is, whether this is a matter as to which the majority of the shareholders can bind those shareholders who dissent. The articles of association constitute a contract not merely between the shareholders and the company, but between each individual shareholder and every other; and the question which I have just stated must in my opinion be answered in the negative if there be in the articles a contract between the shareholders as to the division of profits and the provisions of that contract have not been followed.

Salmon v Quin & Axtens Ltd (1909) CA

The defendant company's articles of association provided that the board of directors had power to manage the company's business subject to a power of veto by the two joint managing directors over certain categories of decision. One of the joint managing directors, Mr Salmon, sought to exercise this power of veto he enjoyed under the articles over a particular board resolution and he sued the company to enforce compliance with his veto.

Held His action succeeded. Farwell LJ cited with approval the words of Stirling J in *Wood v Odessa Waterworks Co* extracted above. He said that the board resolutions which were in dispute and that Mr Salmon was attempting to block were absolutely inconsistent with the power of veto conferred on Mr Salmon by the articles:

> ... [I]n truth, this is an attempt to alter the terms of the contract between the parties by a simple resolution instead of by a special resolution. The articles forming this contract, under which the business of the company shall be managed by the board, contain a most usual and proper requirement, because a business does require a head to look after it ...

Hickman v Kent or Romney Marsh Sheep-Breeders' Association (1915)

The defendant was a non-profit-making company which numbered the plaintiff, Hickman, among its members. The defendant's articles contained an arbitration clause whereby all the members agreed to submit any dispute relating to the affairs of the association or any question of construction of the articles to independent arbitration. A dispute arose between Hickman and the defendant company. He feared expulsion by the defendant and he applied to court for an injunction to prevent that possibility and the defendant company countered with proceedings to stay Hickman's action and to refer the dispute to arbitration in accordance with its articles.

Held Hickman was bound by the articles to submit to arbitration. Articles of association which regulate the rights and obligations of members have the legal effect of creating rights and obligations between the members and the company respectively. However articles of association only bind and confer rights on members of the company not on persons who are 'outsiders' to the company in the sense of not being members.

Rayfield v Hands (1960)

The articles of association of a private company contained the proviso that any member who intended to transfer his shares must inform the directors who would purchase that member's shares equally at a fair value. The plaintiff wished to sell his shares and attempted to enforce the articles against the three directors of the company. However the directors were refusing to purchase his shares in accordance with the articles. The question for the court was did the articles create an obligation incumbent on these directors to so purchase the plaintiff's shares?

Held The plaintiff succeeded in enforcing the articles directly against the directors. The articles served to create a contractual relationship between the plaintiff as shareholder and vendor and the defendants as directors and purchasers. Vaisey J dealt with the problems raised by the reasoning of the courts examined below, 4.1.3 by saying:

> Now the question arises at the outset whether the terms of [the] article ... relate to the rights of the members *inter se* ... or whether the relationship is between a member as such and directors as such. I may dispose of this point very briefly by saying that, in my judgment, the relationship here is between the plaintiff as a member and the defendants not as directors but as members.

He laid great emphasis on this company's characteristics as a quasi-partnership company and the fact that the directors were working members who owned all of the company's shares between them.

4.1.3 Articles of association and the enforcement of outsider rights

Eley v Positive Government Security Life Assurance Co Ltd (1876) CA

The plaintiff, Eley, was a solicitor and keen to act as the defendant company's solicitor. Upon its formation, the defendant company's articles of association named Eley as the company's solicitor. He was never formally appointed solicitor by the company. However, he had acted in that capacity and when the company dispensed with his services he sued it for breach of contract basing his action on the article of association which named him as solicitor to the company.

Held The claim failed since the articles are simply a contract between the shareholders *inter se* and cannot give a right of action to someone who is not a party to the articles. This is so even if the articles name him and attempt to confer rights and obligations upon him. In that he is not a member he is an 'outsider' to the company and no article can, in itself, constitute a contract between the company and such an outsider.

Beattie v E & F Beattie Ltd (1938) CA

The plaintiff was a minority shareholder in the defendant company. A co-defendant in this action was Ernest Beattie who was a director and also a member of E & F Beattie Ltd. The articles of association contained an arbitration clause which provided that any dispute between members of the company or between the company and any member which touched on the conduct of the company's business or any act or default of the directors should be referred to independent arbitration rather than being the subject of legal proceedings. The plaintiff became suspicious about the level of remuneration paid to Ernest Beattie and another director and brought an action against Ernest Beattie for breach of fiduciary duty owed to the company as a director. Ernest Beattie sought to strike out the plaintiff's action against him by arguing that it was in contravention of the arbitration article of association. He claimed to be able to enforce the arbitration article against the plaintiff in spite of the fact that he was being sued in his capacity as a director or 'outsider' to use the terminology employed in *Hickman's* case and *Eley* (above). He argued that although apparently a defendant in these proceedings in an outsider capacity he was also a member of E & F Beattie Ltd and it was in this capacity, as a member, that he sought to enforce the relevant article to have the dispute referred to arbitration.

Held This argument, and Ernest Beattie's application to strike out, failed. The Court of Appeal said:

> He is not seeking to enforce a right to call on the company to arbitrate a dispute which is only accidentally a dispute with himself. He is asking, as a disputant, to have the dispute to which he is a party referred.

The court did not accept that the right to have the dispute referred to arbitration under the article which Ernest Beattie was seeking to enforce was a general right of a member as a member. It all stemmed from his actions in an outsider capacity, as a director, and it was in this capacity that the original claim against him arose.

4.1.4 Terms of articles can form part of separate contract

R v New British Iron Co ex p Beckwith (1898)

The action was brought by directors who had worked for the company as such for quite some time. However none of the directors had a written service contract with the company. The articles of association did however provide that the remuneration of the board should be £1,000 pa. The company went into liquidation and the liquidator argued that the directors were not entitled to any arrears of remuneration since the article of association did not have any contractual effect as between the company and the directors.

Held Although the article of association did not in and of itself entitle the directors to remuneration it did, however, constitute a term of a distinct separate service contract between the directors and the company. The court inferred such a contract from the fact that the directors must reasonably have accepted office and acted in that office on the strength of that article. Hence, the article had a two-fold significance in law, both as evidence of the existence of a separate contract and also as a term to be incorporated into that contract.

Swabey v Port Darwin Gold Mining Co (1889) CA

The articles of association of the defendant company provided that the directors be paid £200 pa. The directors acted as such for some time, being paid at this rate. The company then altered its articles to so as to cut the rate to £5 pa. One director, Swabey, immediately resigned his office upon this alteration and claimed arrears of payment at the rate of £200 pa since he had not been paid for the three months prior to the alteration. The company refused his claim for arrears arguing that he could not base a claim on that article as he had no standing to enforce the article since he was an outsider and the article purported to confer rights on him as an outsider.

Held The Court of Appeal agreed with the general proposition about outsider rights under articles of association but they allowed Swabey's claim for arrears at the pre-alteration rate of £200 pa. Swabey may not have enjoyed rights to remuneration under the articles but he did have rights under a separately existing contract of service which could be inferred from the act that he took up his directorship and acted as director with that article (entitling him to £200 pa) before him. Hence, it was incorporated into that contract. The court added the caveat that 'The Director in this position has also as an implied term of that contract the stipulation that his employer can alter the terms on which he serves and if he does so the director can either stay and work for the new rate or leave'. However, the effect of such an alteration is immediate and prospective – it cannot retrospectively take away contractual rights which have already accrued.

4.2   Alteration of the articles

4.2.1   Alteration by the court

Scott v Frank F Scott (London) Ltd (1940) CA

The plaintiff was the widow and executrix of the late Frank Scott. He owned 100 shares in the defendant company at the time of his death. His widow applied to court for a declaration that, on the true construction of the defendant company's articles of association, she was entitled to be registered as the owner of these 100 shares and she sought rectification of the company's register of members to that effect. The defendants counterclaimed with an assertion that she was not so entitled and that in fact a true construction of the company's articles of association meant that she must offer the shares to the co-defendants – her two brothers-in-law who were the only other shareholders in the company. They argued in the alternative that even if the court disagreed with this construction of the articles as they stood then the court should rectify the articles so as to include such a provision affecting the shares of a deceased member.

Held The plaintiff's action succeeded and the defendants' attempt to persuade the court to re-write the articles failed. Luxmoore LJ said:

> it seems to us that there is no room in the case of a company incorporated under the appropriate statute or statutes for the application to either the memorandum or articles of association of the principles upon which a court of equity permits rectification of documents whether *inter partes* or not ...

4.2.2   Restrictions on the ability of the company to effect alteration

Allen v Gold Reefs of West Africa Ltd (1900) CA
The company's articles of association were altered in such a way as to give the company a lien for debts owing from a member over all shares held by that member. Previous to the alteration the company could do this only in respect of partly paid shares. Now this alteration in fact only affected one shareholder, Mr Allen, as he had both fully and partly paid shares. The company exercised a lien over all of his shares including those which had been fully paid up. He challenged the alteration of the articles which empowered them to do this.

Held The alteration stood and in so ruling the Court of Appeal made the following two points. (1) The s 9 power to alter the articles must be exercised *bona fide* for the benefit of the company as a whole. So long as the alteration is so made, it is valid and binding on all members and can alter their existing rights. (2) However, if the alteration is inconsistent with an independent contract between the company and a particular shareholder, then the company cannot rely on the alteration as a defence to a breach of contract. (See further, 4.2.3 below.)

Greenhalgh v Arderne Cinemas Ltd (1951) CA
The articles of association of the defendant company provided for a pre-emptive right for existing members to buy out one of their number who wished to sell his shares in the company. The managing director had negotiated the sale of a controlling interest of shares with an outsider. In order to enable this share sale to take place and to by pass the existing members' pre-emptive rights, a special resolution was passed which provided that any member who wished at any time to sell his shares in the defendant company could do so direct to an outsider provided that the proposed transferee was approved by an ordinary resolution of the company. The

plaintiff sought a declaration that this was invalid as it was not passed *bona fide* and in the interests of the company as a whole.

Held The Court of Appeal affirmed the lower court's refusal to make such a declaration. Evershed MR opined upon the meaning of the phrase '*bona fide* for the benefit of the company as a whole'. He thought that a special resolution of this kind would fail the test if it discriminated between the majority and the minority shareholders so as to afford the majority an advantage over the minority. This special resolution did not do that. The plaintiff's other argument was that the resolution deprived him and other minority shareholders of their existing pre-emptive rights under the articles. To this Evershed MR replied:

> I think that the answer is that when a man comes into a company, he is not entitled to assume that the articles will always remain in a particular form; and that so long as the proposed alteration does not unfairly discriminate [between majority and minority] it is not an objection, provided that the resolution is passed *bona fide*, that the right to tender for the majority holding of shares would be lost by the lifting of the restriction.

Punt v Symons & Co Ltd (1903)

The defendant company's articles gave GG Symons and after his death his executors the power of appointment and removal of directors. When the company had bought GG Symon's business, it had included in that purchase contract a promise not to alter these articles. GG Symons died and disputes arose between his executors and the remaining directors. The directors proposed to alter by way of special resolution the articles which empowered the executors. The executors sought an injunction to prevent this on, *inter alia*, the grounds that the company had undertaken in a separate contract not to so alter its articles.

Held This argument failed. A company cannot contract out of its statutory right to alter its articles although an alteration of articles will not provide a defence to an action against that company for breach of contract.

(Note the injunction was actually granted on the grounds that the directors had improperly exercised their power to issue shares in order to secure passing of the resolution.)

Russell v Northern Bank Development Corporation Ltd (1992) HL

The first defendant had lent monies to two loss-making companies. A restructuring vested control of the two companies in a newly formed holding company which was to be managed by the plaintiff and three other executives. These four were allotted 20 shares each of the holding company's 1,000 shares; a further 120 shares were allotted to the first defendant. The four executives and the holding company agreed by way of a shareholders agreement, which was expressed to take precedence over the articles, that no further share capital would be created or issued in the holding company without the unanimous written consent of the parties to the agreement. The board of the holding company subsequently planned to increase the nominal capital and the plaintiff sought to restrain this on the basis that it would constitute a breach of the agreement.

Held A provision in a company's articles which purports to restrict its statutory power to alter its articles is invalid. A requirement for the unanimous consent of shareholders to an alteration of articles is invalid be it inserted in the memorandum, articles or in a separate agreement. However, an agreement between the shareholders to vote in a particular fashion on a resolution to alter the memorandum or articles is valid even if the effect of such an agreement is to require all the members to support such a resolution if it is to succeed.

4.2.3   Effect of alteration on contracts with the company

Southern Foundries Ltd v Shirlaw (1940) HL

Shirlaw had been appointed managing director of Southern Foundries Ltd in 1933 pursuant to a written agreement. Southern Foundries Ltd was taken over by Federated Industries Ltd in 1936. Southern Foundries Ltd subsequently altered its articles of associations to insert a new article which empowered Federated Industries Ltd, by written instrument, to remove any of its directors. In 1937 Federated Industries Ltd removed Shirlaw from the board of directors pursuant to the new power. Shirlaw sued Southern Foundries Ltd for breach of contract.

Held His action was successful and he was awarded damages. Lord Porter stated as a matter of general principle:

> A company cannot be precluded from altering its articles thereby giving itself power to act upon the provisions of its altered articles – but so to act may nevertheless be a breach of contract if it is contrary to a stipulation validly made before the alteration. Nor can an injunction be granted to prevent the adoption of the new articles and in that sense they are binding on all and sundry, but for the company to act upon them will none the less render it liable in damages if such action is contrary to the previous engagements of the company.

Baily v British Equitable Assurance Co (1904) CA

The plaintiff, Baily, was a policyholder with the defendant company (which was a deed of settlement company) but was not a shareholder therein. When he had taken out his policy the company's byelaws provided for distribution of profits to policyholders with no deductions therefrom. It was now proposed to incorporate the company under the Companies Act and register articles of association which differed from the byelaws in that they would create a sinking fund into which a percentage of profits would be added. The plaintiff applied for a declaration that this requirement in the new articles did not affect his policy, to which profits should still be attributed without any deduction.

Held The Court of Appeal granted the declaration sought. They attached significance to the fact that Baily was not a shareholder but was an independent contractor with the company. Cozens-Hardy LJ said:

> The rights of a shareholder in respect of his shares, except so far as may be protected by the memorandum of association, are by statute made liable to be altered by special resolution. (See *Allen v Gold Reefs of West Africa Ltd.*)

> But the case of a contract between an outsider and the company is entirely different, and even a shareholder must be regarded as an outsider in so far as he contracts with the company otherwise than in respect of his shares. It would be dangerous to hold that in a contract of insurance validly entered into by a company there is any greater power of variation of the rights and liabilities of the parties than would exist if, instead of the company, the contracting party had been an individual. A company cannot, by altering its articles, justify a breach of contract ...

Swabey v Port Darwin Gold Mining Co (1889) CA
Noted, 4.1.4 above.

5 Company directors

5.1 Appointment

5.1.1 Appointment of managing director

Harold Holdsworth & Co (Wakefield) Ltd v Caddies (1955) HL
The respondent, Mr Caddies, had been appointed, for five years, managing director of the appellant company pursuant to an agreement which required him to perform the duties and exercise the powers in relation to the appellant company and the businesses of its subsidiary companies which were assigned to or vested in him by the appellant company's board of directors. Following differences arising between Mr Caddies and the rest of the board of the appellant company the board resolved that he confine his attention solely to the running of the business of one of the appellant's subsidiary companies. Mr Caddies claimed that this was a repudiation of the agreement by which he was appointed managing director by the appellant company.

Held The House of Lords said that it was not a repudiation by the appellant company, indeed the agreement appointing Mr Caddies entitled them to vary the nature of his duties. The office of managing director was not a fixed term of art in company law but depended upon the terms of the individual appointment.

Freeman & Lockyer v Buckhurst Park Properties Ltd (1964) CA
The defendant company was a property development company and had been formed by Mr K and Mr H. These two gentlemen along with two of their nominees constituted the board of directors and all four needed to be present in order for a board meeting to be quorate. Despite the fact that he had contributed half of its capital, Mr H played no active role in the running of the company and was mostly abroad. The running of the company's business was left to Mr K who, although he had never been formally appointed managing director, acted as such. Mr K commissioned the

plaintiff firm of architects to lodge a planning application in respect of a site owned by the company. The company refused payment of the plaintiff's fee on the grounds that Mr K had no authority to engage them on behalf of the company.

Held The Court of Appeal found for the plaintiffs and held that the acts of Mr K did bind the company since the board of directors, in which was vested full powers of management under the articles, knew Mr K had been acting as managing director, and in that they permitted him to do so they represented by conduct that he had the authority of a managing director and the plaintiffs were thus induced to believe that he could so act. Mr K had implied actual authority to act as he did.

Hely-Hutchinson v Brayhead Ltd (1968) CA

Mr Richards was chairman and chief executive of the defendant company but had not been formally appointed managing director or been given express authority to bind the company. However, he acted as managing director and it was quite usual for him to make deals on behalf of the company and tell his fellow directors later. They acquiesced in this practice. The plaintiff was chairman and managing director of another company which it was planned to merge with the defendant company. Mr Richards gave the plaintiff certain letters which committed the defendant company to guarantee payments owing to the plaintiff and to indemnify him against certain losses. The defendant company now claimed that Mr Richards had no authority to commit the company thus.

Held The plaintiff's claim succeeded as Mr Richards was held to have implied actual authority to enter into these commitments on behalf of the defendant company. The board's conduct in its acquiescence to the way in which Mr Richards did business unilaterally on their behalf without their prior sanction was evidence of such implied authority.

5.1.2 Remuneration

Re George Newman and Co (1895) CA

The chairman of a company owned, along with other family members, nearly all the shares in the company. The chairman bought a building agreement on behalf of the company from certain commissioners. These commissioners did not wish the company to be the tenant but preferred the chairman himself as tenant. He then sold the benefit of the agreement to the company for £10,000. Of this, £7,000 was attributable to commissions on the obtaining of the agreement from the commissioners and £3,000 was applied to his own use. A further £3,500 of the company's money was applied by the chairman on his private residence. All this money came from sums borrowed by the company for the purposes of its business and the payments to the chairman had been sanctioned by the directors and all the shareholders. The articles of the company, however, contained no provision to make presents to directors. Upon the winding up of the company the liquidator applied for repayment of these sums from the chairman.

Held Lindley LJ giving the judgment of the Court of Appeal held that the chairman was liable to repay the £3,000 and £3,500 sums. He said in the course of his judgment, that 'Directors have no right to be paid for their services, and cannot pay themselves or each other, or make presents to themselves out of the company's assets, unless authorised to do so by the instrument which regulates the company or by the shareholders at a properly convened meeting. The shareholders at a meeting duly convened for the purpose, can, if they think proper, remunerate directors for their trouble or make presents to them for their services out of assets properly divisible amongst the shareholders themselves ...'.

Craven Ellis v Canons Ltd (1936) CA

The plaintiff had been purportedly appointed managing director of the defendant company by an agreement which set out a rate of remuneration payable but was in actual fact void as the directors of the company were not qualified to act as such under the articles. The company now relied on this want of authority in the plaintiff's appointment in its refusal to pay him for the services of managing director which had already rendered to the company.

Held Despite the fact that his appointment as managing director was void the plaintiff was still entitled to payment on a *quantum meruit* basis.

Re Richmond Gate Property Ltd (1964)

The company's articles provided that its managing director was entitled to such remuneration as the directors may determine. The company went into liquidation having not paid its managing director and without the directors having considered the matter of his payment.

Held His claim for payment on a *quantum meruit* basis failed since the judge said there was express provision for remuneration which had simply not been employed by the company.

Re Halt Garage (1964) Ltd (1982)

Mr and Mrs C were the sole directors of the company and owned all its shares. They both worked in the business, drawing directors' remuneration as authorised to do under the company's constitution. However, Mrs C became ill in 1967 and withdrew from involvement in the company's business. She continued to be a director and received payment as such at a reduced rate. By 1968 the company was no longer profitable and it went into insolvent liquidation in 1971. The liquidator applied for repayment of sums allegedly overpaid to Mr and Mrs C as directors' remuneration. He argued that Mrs C should not have been entitled to any remuneration from the time she became ill onwards and that the level of Mr C's remuneration was unreasonable and disproportionate to the benefit gained by the company in the light of the company's unprofitability.

Held The liquidator's claim against Mr C failed as the court thought that it was not for the courts to pronounce on the level of directors' remuneration but rather this was a question for the shareholders and in the absence of fraud or of the company making a distribution of its capital then although the law required shareholders to be honest it did not require them to be wise in setting the level of directors' remuneration.

However, the court agreed with the liquidator with regard to those sums paid to Mrs C, ostensibly as remuneration, after she had become ill and withdrawn from active participation in the company. This, said the court, was not genuine remuneration but was a disguised gift of capital and thus repayable to the company.

Guinness plc v Saunders (1990) HL

In 1986 Guinness plc launched a contested takeover bid for the Distillers brewing group. During the course of its bid Guinness formed an executive committee of its directors Mr Roux, Mr Saunders and Mr Ward known as 'the war cabinet'. Mr Ward was a US lawyer and all three were members of the board of directors of Guinness plc. A Jersey-based company owned by Mr Ward provided consultancy advice to Guinness during the bid and was paid a fee of £5.2 million. This fee had, allegedly, been agreed by the war cabinet, but not by the main board of Guinness. Indeed, the main Board of directors was not appraised of this payment at all. Guinness sought repayment of this fee on the grounds that the failure to disclose to the board the payment to one of the directors was a breach of fiduciary duty on the part of Mr Ward. He in turn tried to argue that it was remuneration which he was entitled to under Guinness plc's articles of association.

Held The House of Lords held that the contract to pay Mr Ward was void and he was not entitled to keep this sum. Guinness' articles of association did not empower the 'war cabinet' to approve this payment as special remuneration. Neither could Mr Ward rely on another of Guinness' articles which entitled a director acting in another professional capacity to be remunerated as such for work undertaken in that capacity. Mr Ward had no other general right to remuneration and, unless he could point to some provision in Guinness' articles entitling him to this sum as special remuneration, then he must be presumed to have acted gratuitously on Guinness' behalf.

5.2 Removal

Bushell v Faith (1970) HL

The company had 300 shares issued. The plaintiff, defendant and their sister held 100 each. The plaintiff and the defendant were the only directors. The company's articles of association weighted the voting rights attached to the shares from the normal one vote per share to three votes per share where, and only where, the issue before a general meeting of the company was the removal of the director holding those shares. The plaintiff and her sister tried to remove the defendant from office as a director. The issue thus arose as to whether a court should give effect to the weighted voting rights attached by the articles to the defendant's shares which would, if recognised, have the effect of blocking the resolution to remove him by 300 votes to 200.

Held The House of Lords decided to recognise the weighted voting rights accorded by the articles. In so doing they drew a distinction between the voting rights attached to shares and the mandatory scope of s 303 of the Companies Act 1985. They thought that Parliament, in enacting s 303, did not mean to fetter the scope for a company to issue a share with such rights or restrictions attaching to the share as the company saw fit.

Re BML Group Ltd (1994) CA

A shareholders' agreement was in existence and it provided that a meeting of the company was only quorate if B or his proxy were present at it. A resolution to remove B as a director was passed at a meeting in his absence and he brought a s 459 action in protest at his removal.

Held The Court of Appeal upheld the effect of the shareholder's agreement saying that B's rights were in effect class rights which could not be overridden. They had the same effect as if they were class rights contained in the company's articles of association.

5.3   Disqualification

Re Keypak Homecare Ltd (1990)

The Secretary of State for Trade and Industry applied under s 6 of the Company Directors Disqualification Act (CDDA) 1986 for disqualification orders against the two directors of Keypak Homecare Ltd on the grounds of their unfitness. The company ceased trading in October 1996 and at that point its two directors set up a new company which bought Keypak Ltd's stock for a very low price. Only after its assets had been taken over by the new company did Keypak Ltd go into liquidation, in December 1986. The factors the Secretary of State used to found his allegation of unfitness were: (1) The directors had paid themselves excessive remuneration at a time when they knew the company was doing badly. (2) Just prior to its liquidation Keypak had repaid a loan to one of its directors. (3) The Directors had retained Crown monies (VAT, PAYE contributions, etc). (4) The Directors had sold the stock of Keypak Ltd to the new company at considerably less than it was worth.

Held The disqualification order was granted. The court thought the first two factors did not indicate a want of commercial probity on the part of the directors, and that the lack of probity attaching to the third factor was not, in the circumstances, sufficiently serious to justify disqualification for unfitness. However, the court thought that the sale of stock from Keypak Ltd to the new company did display, on the part of the directors, a serious want of commercial probity so as to render them unfit to be directors of a company.

Re Sevenoaks Stationers (Retail) Ltd (1991) CA

Mr C was a chartered accountant and a director of several companies, all of which had become insolvent. At first instance, the court declared him 'unfit to be concerned in the management of a company' within the meaning of s 6 of the CDDA 1986 having heard that he had failed to keep, prepare and file proper accounting records and annual reports, failed to pay tax monies due to the Crown, and caused the companies to incur further indebtedness when he knew or ought to have known that they were in great difficulties and had caused the companies to trade whilst insolvent.

Held The Court of Appeal imposed a five-year disqualification order and enunciated some guidelines for the operation of the Act's jurisdiction. Dillon LJ approved the division of the potential 15-year disqualification under the CDDA 1986 into three tiers. He said the top tier of disqualification periods over 10 years should be reserved for the most serious of cases such as the director who has already had one ban imposed on him and incurs another. The middle tier, six to 10 years should be used where the case is serious but falls short of the top tier and the minimum tariff of two to five years should be used where, although disqualification is mandatory, the case is relatively not very serious.

Secretary of State for Trade and Industry v Tjolle and others (1997)

This was an application for disqualification of Mrs Diana Kenning who had been an employee of Land Travel Ltd, a holiday company which had gone into liquidation with debts of over £12 million in 1992. The main shareholder and director of Land Travel Ltd, Mr Tjolle, had been guilty of fraudulent trading and had agreed to a maximum disqualification order of 15 years. It was alleged that Mrs Kenning had acted as a *de facto* director and therefore ought to be disqualified pursuant to s6 of the CDDA 1986.

Held The disqualification proceedings against Mrs Kenning failed. The court said that the essential purpose of a disqualification order was to protect the public and that purpose was not served in this case. Any side effects of a disqualification order such as heavy costs penalties, stigma and deterrence should not form the Secretary of State's motivation for bringing and maintaining disqualification proceedings. The court also emphasised the importance of both civil and criminal courts adhering to the guidelines for disqualification periods laid down in *Re Sevenoaks Stationers (Retail) Ltd* when considering applications under s 6 of the CDDA 1986.

5.4 Powers of directors

5.4.1 Division of powers between the directors and the company in general meeting

Automatic Self-Cleansing Filter Syndicate Co Ltd v Cunninghame (1906) CA
By its articles of association, the general management and control of the plaintiff company were vested in the directors, subject to such regulations as might be made from time to time by extraordinary resolution. At a general meeting of the company, a resolution was passed by a simple majority of the shareholders for the sale of the company's assets on certain terms, directing the directors to carry the sale into effect. The directors of the company declined to comply with the resolution, being of the opinion that a sale on those terms was not for the benefit of the company. Mr M, on behalf of himself and all the other shareholders of the plaintiff company, brought a motion against the defendant directors, asking that they be ordered to comply with the resolution.

Held The articles of association determined which organ had the power of management and as such the directors could not be compelled to comply with the resolution, which conflicted with the provisions of the articles.

Quin & Axtens Ltd v Salmon (1909) HL
The articles of association of the appellant company vested in the directors the general management of the company. With regard to certain matters, however, the articles provided that no resolution of the directors should be valid if either of the two managing directors dissented. The respondent, one of the two managing directors, so dissented from such a resolution. At an extraordinary general meeting, the company purported to ratify the original resolution by a simple majority. The respondent, as original plaintiff, was granted an injunction restraining the company from acting on the resolutions of the board and the general meeting. The company appealed.

Held The House of Lords dismissed the appeal. The resolutions were inconsistent with the provisions of the articles and the company was properly restrained from acting thereon. The right of management veto, as contained in the articles, was therefore upheld.

John Shaw & Sons (Salford) Ltd v Shaw (1935) CA
The defendants were directors of, and were indebted to, the plaintiff company. Terms of settlement were reached concerning their debts, and under which they became ordinary directors of the company. The articles of association were altered so as to vest the general power of management in newly-appointed permanent directors. An agreement containing the terms of settlement was sealed by the company. The defendants declined to execute the agreement, whereupon the permanent directors resolved to institute proceedings in the company's name against the defendants for recovery

of the debts. The company in general meeting resolved to discontinue the proceedings.

Held The Court of Appeal declared the resolution of the company to be invalid. The general power of management being vested in the permanent directors by the articles, they and they alone could exercise those powers, including the power to litigate. Any decision by the permanent directors could not be overridden by the mere resolution of the company in general meeting. Greer LJ emphasised that the company was an entity distinct alike from its shareholders and its directors. According to the company's articles, certain powers could be delegated to the directors or be reserved for the company in general meeting. If a power was vested in the directors, the shareholders could not usurp its use by them. The only way the general body of shareholders could control the exercise of powers vested in the directors would be to alter the articles or, if the opportunity arose, to refuse to re-elect directors if they disapproved of their actions.

Barron v Potter (1914)

The parties were sole directors of a company. The articles of association of that company gave the directors the power to appoint an additional director. Owing to differences between the two directors, no board meeting could be held for the purpose of such an appointment.

Held If a situation existed in which there was, for all practical purposes, no board of directors at all, there was a residual power of management in the company in general meeting. Warrington J stated, in the course of his judgment, 'If directors having certain powers are unable or unwilling to exercise them – are in fact a non-existent body for the purpose – there must be some power in the company to do itself that which under other circumstances would be otherwise done'.

Alexander Ward & Co v Samyang Navigation Co (1975) HL

By the articles of association of the respondent company, the power of management was vested in the board of directors. At the relevant time, there were no directors of the company. Proceedings were brought against the appellants by W and I, both members of the respondent company, in the company's name. The respondent company went into liquidation and, through its liquidator, purported to ratify the acts of W and I.

Held The company was, at the relevant time, competent to bring proceedings. The House of Lords decided that the company in general meeting had, in the absence of an effective board, a residual authority to use the company's powers. The company having gone into liquidation, the acts of W and I were validly ratified by the company through the liquidator, and those acts were thus valid from the first.

Re Argentum Reductions (UK) Ltd (1975)

The company had two directors, and its voting shares were held by their respective wives. The board became deadlocked and the minority shareholder presented a petition for winding up the company. The applicants in the proceedings were the majority shareholder, her husband as one of the directors, and the company. They applied for an order that the company's bank account not be frozen so that debts incurred after the date of the petition could be duly paid. The court was asked a preliminary point as to whether the applicants had *locus standi* to make the application.

Held The shareholder had a discernible interest in the matter in that, although not normally a party to the transaction, it may closely affect the value of her shares, and thus she had an interest to protect, even if indirect. On the issue of the division of powers, Megarry J stated: 'If one accepts to the full that the shareholders cannot reverse a decision of the directors, or compel them to do what they do not want to do, one does not necessarily reach the conclusion that where the directors are in deadlock as to a course of action, the majority of shareholders are powerless to come down on one side or the other. Nevertheless, there are deep waters here'. His Lordship refused to come to a decision on the point.

Mitchell & Hobbs (UK) Ltd v Mill (1995)

Mr Radford was the managing director and major shareholder of the plaintiff which was a small private company. The other director was Mr Pearce – there were only two directors and the company had adopted articles 70 and 72 of Table A in its articles of association. Mr Radford initiated legal proceedings in the name of the company against the company's secretary, Mr Mill. He took this step with no reference to his fellow director, Mr Pearce – there was no meeting of the board authorising the proceedings.

Held The legal proceedings were struck out as they were unauthorised. Articles 70 and 72 of Table A did not empower a single director to authorise the bringing of legal proceedings without reference to his fellow directors. To hold otherwise would allow for the undesirable possibility of multiple legal proceedings being brought in the name of a company some of which some directors would be ignorant of. Article 70 must be construed in such a way as to mean the power to manage the company is a power to be exercised by the board of directors, not a single director acting as the board of directors. The fact that Mr Radford was a managing director made no difference in itself – the Articles gave the board of directors power to delegate special powers (including the power to instigate litigation) to the managing director but no such delegation had taken place in this case.

5.4.2   Directors' authority to bind the company

Royal British Bank v Turquand (Turquand's Case) (1856)

The Royal British Bank sued Turquand as the liquidator of a mining and railway company for the repayment of £2,000 borrowed on a bond signed by the company's two directors and its secretary. Under the company's constitution the directors' power to borrow money was limited by the requirement that the amount of such sums as were from time to time required had first to be authorised by ordinary resolution of the company. This requirement had not been fulfilled. The company argued that the bond was thus invalid.

Held Third parties (ie the Royal British Bank) were bound to read the constitution of the company but thereafter were not obliged to inquire into the proceedings of the company. Instead they had a right to infer that all acts of internal management had been properly carried out, unless the third party knew or ought to have known of the failure to adhere to the procedures. The constitution gave the directors the power to borrow money, subject to certain internal procedures. The Royal British Bank were entitled to assume that all these procedures had been properly adhered to. The bond was thus valid and the bank were entitled to repayment thereof.

Mahony v East Holyford Mining Co (1875)

The respondent company was incorporated and its memorandum and articles of association duly registered. The appellant represented the respondent company's bank. The bank received notice of a 'resolution' purporting to appoint three named persons as directors of the company, and one as secretary, upon whose authority cheques could be drawn. The bank from time to time received cheques signed in accordance with the notice, and duly honoured them. The company was then ordered to be wound up. It transpired that there had neither been a meeting of shareholders nor any appointment of directors or a secretary. The named persons had merely treated themselves as such. The official liquidator attempted to recover from the bank the amount of the cheques paid.

Held The appeal was allowed. The official liquidator could not recover from the bank. The bank was not bound to inquire whether the persons pretending to sign as directors had been duly appointed. Lord Hatherley stated: 'Where there are persons conducting the affairs of the company in a manner which appears to be perfectly consonant with the articles of association, then those so dealing with them, externally, are not to be affected by any irregularities in the internal management of the company.'

Freeman & Lockyer v Buckhurst Park Properties (Mangal) (1964)
See above, p 39.

Hely-Hutchinson v Brayhead Ltd (1968) CA
See above, p 40.

5.4.3 Directors to use powers for proper purpose

Punt v Symons & Co Ltd (1903)

The articles of association of the defendant company gave to the governing director, S, the power to appoint and remove directors. After the death of S, the power became exercisable by his executors. Friction arose between S's executors and the directors. The directors of the company issued shares for the purpose of creating a sufficient majority to enable them to pass a special resolution to alter the company's articles and deprive the executors of this power. The plaintiff objected to the directors' use of their power to issue shares. The directors asserted that they honestly believed the share issue to be in the best interests of the company.

Held Where shares had been issued by the directors for some purpose other than for the benefit of the company, the transaction was liable to be set aside, and the directors restrained from holding the meeting at which the votes of the new shareholders were to be used. The power was given primarily for the purpose of enabling the directors to raise capital when required by the company. However, Byrne J added that: 'There may be occasions when the directors may fairly and properly issue shares ... for other reasons. For instance, it would not be at all an unreasonable thing to create a sufficient number of shareholders to enable statutory powers to be exercised; but when I find a limited issue of shares to persons who are obviously meant and intended to secure the necessary statutory majority in a particular interest, I do not think that it is a fair and *bona fide* exercise of the power.'

Hogg v Cramphorn Ltd (1967)

The defendant company was the subject of a takeover bid by B. The directors of the company acting in good faith believed the takeover not to be in the best interests of the company or its staff. The directors therefore devised a scheme under which 10 votes per share on a poll were attached to 5,707 unissued preference shares. These shares were allotted to trustees for the company's employees, and interest-free loans advanced to the trustees in order for them to pay for the shares. The purported effect of the transactions was that the directors could rely on the support of the majority of the total votes, thus preventing the takeover by B. The plaintiff, a shareholder in the defendant company and an associate of B, challenged the transactions.

Held The power to issue shares was a fiduciary power and must be exercised for a proper purpose or the issue was liable to be set aside, notwithstanding that the issue was made in the *bona fide* belief that it was in the interests of the company. The primary purpose of the scheme was to ensure control of the company by the directors and their supporters, which was an improper purpose. The transactions were, therefore, liable to be set aside. (The case was adjourned and the transactions were subsequently ratified by the original shareholders.)

Bamford v Bamford (1970) CA

The defendant company had an authorised share capital of £1,000,000 divided into 5,000,000 shares, 4,500,000 of which were issued. Upon receiving a takeover bid, the company purported to issue the 500,000 unissued shares to another company. The plaintiffs, two shareholders in the defendant company, brought an action against the company claiming the allotment to be invalid in that the directors had acted in bad faith from an improper motive to block the takeover bid. A general meeting of the company's original shareholders was called and the acts of the directors were ratified by resolution. The plaintiffs claimed that this resolution was a nullity. The plaintiffs' action was dismissed and they appealed.

Held The Court of Appeal dismissed the appeal, stating that even if the directors could be shown to have acted in bad faith in issuing the shares for the purpose of blocking the takeover bid, any impropriety could be and had been waived by the resolution of the company in general meeting. Even if the allotment was initially voidable, it had been properly ratified by the original shareholders.

Howard Smith v Ampol Petroleum Ltd (1974) PC

Two companies, A (the respondents) and B, owned the majority of the issued share capital of M, a third company. A and H (the appellants) made competing takeover bids for M. The directors of M favoured H's higher bid, but A and B would not accept H's offer. M required further capital. The directors of M decided to allot new shares to H for two purposes, contending that the primary purpose was to raise the required capital, and that the other purpose was to reduce the shareholding of A and B to a minority one to allow H's bid to succeed. A challenged the validity of the allotment. The Supreme Court of New South Wales found the primary purpose to be to reduce the shareholding of A and B and that the allotment was thus for an improper purpose. H appealed.

Held The Privy Council dismissed the appeal on the ground that it was unconstitutional for the directors to use their power to allot shares for the primary purpose (in the opinion of the court) of destroying an existing majority or creating a new majority. The allotment was set aside. The court proffered guidelines as to the proper approach to take in such cases. First, the court must look at the source of the power in order to ascertain its limits. Having so established this, it is necessary to determine the actual purpose for which it was exercised. This actual purpose must then be measured against the permissible purposes for which the power was given. If this actual purpose is a proper one, then it will not be tainted by the presence of some other improper, but insubstantial, purpose.

6 Duties of directors

6.1 To whom are directors' duties owed?

Percival v Wright (1902)

The plaintiffs were the registered owners of shares in a company. Negotiations took place and eventually a sale of the shares was agreed, to the chairman and two other directors of the company. The plaintiffs subsequently learnt that, prior to and during their own negotiations, the board of directors had been approached by a third party with a view to the purchase of the entire undertaking of the company at prices far higher per share than that agreed in the sale. These negotiations ultimately failed. The plaintiffs brought an action against the chairman and the two directors asking to have the sale set aside on the ground that the directors ought to have disclosed the negotiations with the third party for the sale of the company's undertaking.

Held The directors of a company owe fiduciary duties to the company but not to individual shareholders. Since the directors owe no fiduciary duties to the shareholders, they could not be liable for non-disclosure. In the course of his judgment, Swinfen-Eady J stated: 'I am therefore of opinion that the purchasing directors were under no obligation to disclose to their vendor shareholders the negotiations which ultimately proved abortive. The contrary view would place directors in a most invidious position, as they could not buy or sell shares without disclosing negotiations, a premature disclosure of which might well be against the best interests of the company.'

Allen v Hyatt (1914) PC

The appellants were the directors of a company. They represented to the respondents, shareholders in that company, that it was necessary for the directors to secure the consent of the majority of the shareholders in order to effect an amalgamation with another company. The respondents were induced to give the appellants options to purchase their shares. These were exercised and the amalgamation took place, making a profit for the appellants. The respondents, as original plaintiffs, brought an action for a declaration that the appellants were trustees for the shareholders of the profits made.

Held The appellants were trustees of the profits for the benefit of the respondents. The nature of the transaction was such that the directors had effectively been appointed by the shareholders as their agents in the matter. The directors thus owed the shareholders the ordinary fiduciary duties arising from an agency relationship, which included the duty not to make a personal profit from any transaction.

Gething v Kilner (1972)

A takeover bid was agreed between the chairman of TC Ltd and the Rochdale Canal Co that TC Ltd would offer £200 for every £100 of Rochdale stock, on condition that the Rochdale directors would recommend acceptance of the offer. The Rochdale directors then approached a firm of stockbrokers, who advised that the offer was inadequate. The Rochdale directors issued a circular to their stockholders which referred briefly to the conclusion of the stockbrokers, but recommended acceptance of the offer. Four Rochdale stockholders, one of whom had accepted the offer, brought a motion against the Rochdale directors, TC Ltd and the Rochdale Canal Co for an injunction to restrain TC Ltd from declaring their offer unconditional.

Held The motion was dismissed. The directors of an offeree company in a takeover have a duty towards their own shareholders, which includes a duty to be honest and a duty not to mislead. Therefore, a minority group could complain of the directors' actions, but in the absence of bad faith the court would not intervene for fear of upsetting the will of the majority. Brightman J saw 'no sufficient reason why their contract should be placed in peril in the absence of bad faith on the part of the two boards or conduct so unreasonable as to approach bad faith'.

Heron International Ltd v Lord Grade (1983) CA

The directors of the target company of a proposed takeover were faced with two competing bids. The articles of the company gave the directors the power to choose which bid to accept. The directors, for a number of reasons, chose the lower bid. The plaintiffs, suing as representatives of the shareholders in the defendant company, sought an injunction to prevent the transfer.

Held The directors were under a fiduciary obligation to exercise the power to register a proposed transfer in the interests of both the company and the shareholders. The Court of Appeal decided that: 'Where directors have decided that it is in the best interests of a company that the company be taken over and there are two or more bidders the only duty of directors ... is to obtain the best price.' In considering rival bids in a takeover the interests of the company were the interests of the current shareholders. The injunction was therefore granted.

6.2 Common law duties

Re City Equitable Fire & Insurance Co Ltd (1925)

The company had experienced a serious depletion of funds and was in the process of being wound up by the court. The managing director had been convicted of fraud, and the liquidator sought to make other directors liable in negligence for failing to detect the frauds.

Held The other directors were not liable. Romer J set out the general duties of care and skill attributed to directors:

> There are, in addition, one or two other general propositions that seem to be warranted by the reported cases:
>
> (1) A director need not exhibit in the performance of his duties a greater degree of skill than may reasonably be expected from a person of his knowledge and experience ...
>
> (2) A director is not bound to give continuous attention to the affairs of his company. His duties are of an intermittent nature to be performed at periodic board meetings and at meetings of any committee of the board upon which he happens to be placed. He is not, however, bound to attend all such meetings, though he ought to attend whenever in the circumstances, he is reasonably able to do so.
>
> (3) In respect of all duties that, having regard to the exigencies of business, and the articles of association, may properly be left to some other official, a director is, in the absence of grounds for suspicion, justified in trusting that official to perform such duties honestly ...

Re Denham & Co (1883)

Over a period of four years, annual reports of the company were issued to shareholders purporting to show profits of 15% each year available for payment by dividend, which was duly declared and paid. C was one of the directors but neither attended board meetings nor took part in the preparation or issue of the reports. During the four years, he only occasionally attended the company's general meetings. The company was subsequently ordered to be wound up, and it was found that the dividends for the four years had been paid out of capital and not out of profits. In order to show profits available, the accounts had been fraudulently manipulated without the knowledge of C. Certain creditors issued a summons to compel C to repay the amount of dividends paid out of capital.

Held C was not personally liable for the fraudulent reports and the dividends paid thereunder. He was a country gentleman and not an accountant. He had no reason to suspect any misconduct and was thus not guilty of such negligence so as to render himself personally liable.

Re Cardiff Savings Bank, Marquis of Bute's Case (1892)

The rules of a savings bank were not complied with and the result was the perpetration of frauds upon the bank by its paid officer. The bank was forced to suspend payment. In 38 years as the president and a director of the bank, since his appointment when he was only six months old, the Marquis of Bute had attended only one board meeting and was unaware of the irregularities which had occurred. The liquidator sought to make him liable in the winding up of the bank.

Held The Marquis was not liable. Omission to attend the meetings of the bank was not the same as neglect or omission of the duties which ought to have been performed at such meetings, especially where he had not undertaken to attend. There were a total of 55 managers and trustees of the bank and it could not be expected that each one should take an active part in management or attend every meeting.

Dovey v Cory (1901) HL

The respondent was a director of the National Bank of Wales, which was being wound up. Balance sheets were laid before meetings by the chairman and general manager of the company which were not proper and which did not truly report as to the state and condition of the company and did not comply with the requirements of the articles. Under the pretext that the balance sheets were accurate, the respondent assented to the payment of dividends out of capital and to advances on improper security. The liquidator sought a declaration that the respondent should be held personally liable due to his negligence.

Held On the facts, the respondent was not negligent of his duties and could not be held personally liable in the winding up. He had no reason to doubt the integrity, skill and competence of the chairman and general manager, and therefore his reliance on the balance sheets prepared by them was reasonable. In the course of his judgment, the Earl of Halsbury LC stated: 'I cannot think that it can be expected of a director that he should be watching either the inferior officers of the bank or verifying the calculations of the auditors himself. The business of life could not go on if people could not trust those who are put into a position of trust for the express purpose of attending to details of management.'

Re Brazilian Rubber Plantations & Estates Ltd (1901)

The company was formed in order to purchase certain estates in Brazil. Its directors were all induced to become so by Mr Harbod. None of the directors who undertook the management of the company knew anything of the rubber industry. One consented to act solely because he was assured that the office would give him a little pleasant employment without him incurring any responsibility. One was 75 years old and very deaf. The directors issued a prospectus inviting subscriptions for shares which contained statements which were untrue. These statements were taken from a report given to the directors which was fraudulent, although the directors believed it to be an honest report and did not inquire into its accuracy. Before the whole of the purchase money was paid, the directors learnt of the inaccuracy of the report but went on to complete the purchase. The company was ordered to be wound up and the liquidator took out a summons claiming damages against the directors for gross negligence.

Held The conduct of the directors did not amount to gross negligence. Neville J said:

> A director's duty has been laid down as requiring him to act with such care as is reasonably to be expected from him, having regard to his knowledge and experience. He is, I think, not bound to bring any special qualifications to his office. He may undertake the management of a rubber company in complete ignorance of everything connected with rubber, without incurring responsibility for the mistakes which may occur from such ignorance; while if he is acquainted with the rubber business he must give the company the advantage of his knowledge when transacting the company's business.

Dorchester Finance Co Ltd v Stebbings (1977)

S, P and H were directors of the plaintiff company. S and P were chartered accountants and H had considerable accounting experience. The management of the company was left to S, with P and H fulfilling roles as non-executive directors. As neither P nor H visited the company frequently, they often left signed cheques in blank to be used by S at some later date. Losses were incurred when unsecured loans were made which turned out to be unrecoverable. The plaintiff company brought an action against S, P and H alleging negligence in the management of the company's affairs.

Held Foster J decided that all three were liable in negligence. A director in carrying out his duties was required to exhibit such a degree of skill as may reasonably be expected from a person of his knowledge and experience. No distinction was to be drawn between executive and non-executive directors. The court rejected the argument that non-executive directors could rely on the competence and diligence of the auditors and do nothing themselves, whether they had accounting experience or not.

Norman v Theodore Goddard (1991)

Q was a chartered surveyor with no knowledge of company law or offshore financial matters who was appointed as a director of LB Investments (LBI). B, a partner in Theodore Goddard, suggested that, for tax reasons, substantial sums held in cash by LBI should be invested in an offshore company. B made assurances to Q as to the profitability, availability and security of the funds. The offshore company was in fact controlled by B who stole the money transferred to it by LBI. Theodore Goddard sought a contribution from Q on the basis that he had acted in breach of his duty of care as a director of LBI.

Held Q was not in breach of duty and the claim of Theodore Goddard thus failed. The test of a director's duty was accurately stated in s 214(4) of the Insolvency Act 1986. The relevant test was what could be expected of a person in the position of director carrying out those functions. A director was entitled to trust persons in positions of responsibility until there was reason to distrust them.

Re D'Jan of London Ltd (1993)

The company was insolvent with a deficiency as regards unsecured creditors of around £500,000. D held 99 out of the 100 issued shares of the company. The liquidator claimed that D was negligent in completing and signing a fire insurance form which resulted in the insurers repudiating liability for a fire at the company's premises which caused damage to the extent of £174,000. In his evidence, D said that he did not fill in the form or read it before he signed.

Held In failing to read the form D was negligent. By signing the form, he effectively accepted responsibility for its contents. Hoffman LJ stated that 'the duty of care owed by a director at common law is accurately stated in s 214(4) of the Insolvency Act 1986'. That test was both subjective and objective, and D failed to show reasonable diligence when he signed the form.

6.3 Fiduciary duties

6.3.1 Duty to act *bona fide* in the best interests of the company

Re Smith & Fawcett Ltd (1942)

Smith and Fawcett were the directors and sole shareholders of the company. Fawcett died and Smith and a newly appointed second director refused to register Fawcett's shares in the name of his executor unless he was willing to sell half of them to Smith. The articles of the company stated: 'The directors may at any time and in their absolute and uncontrolled discretion refuse to register any transfer of shares.' The applicant claimed to be registered as the holder of the shares.

Held The Court of Appeal refused to intervene with the exercise of discretion by the directors. The court held that the discretion was subject only to the limitation that it should be exercised *bona fide* in the interests of the company. Lord Greene MR stated, in the course of his judgment: 'They must exercise their discretion in what they consider – not what a court may consider – is in the interests of the company and not for any collateral purpose.' There was no direct evidence that an improper purpose had been considered.

6.3.2 Conflict of duty and interest

Aberdeen Railway Co v Blaikie Bros (1854) HL

The appellant company agreed to buy goods from the respondent partnership. Blaikie was a member of the respondent partnership and was also a director of the appellant company. The company refused to honour the contract and the partnership sought its enforcement.

Held The House of Lords decided that the company were entitled to avoid the contract. There was a clear conflict between Blaikie's duty to secure for the company the lowest possible price, and his interest as a member of the partnership to make the greatest profit, and in such circumstances a contract was unenforceable against the company. Lord Cranworth stated: 'So strictly is this principle adhered to, that no question is allowed to be raised as to the fairness or unfairness of a contract so entered into.'

Regal (Hastings) Ltd v Gulliver (1942) HL

Regal owned one cinema which it wished to sell. The directors decided to acquire two additional cinemas in the name of a subsidiary (Amalgamated) with a view to selling all three as a going concern. The other two cinemas were available on long lease. The issued capital of Amalgamated was £2,000 and unless this was increased to £5,000 the lessor would only grant a lease if the Regal directors guaranteed the rent, which they were not prepared to do. Regal itself could not raise the extra £3,000. In order to raise the £3,000 required, the four directors of Regal put up £500 apiece, with other investors contributing the remaining finance. Amalgamated then acquired the leases. The directors of Regal then sold their shares in Regal and Amalgamated at a profit. Regal sued the directors for the profit.

Held The directors were liable to account for the profit they made on the resale of their shares notwithstanding that Regal could not have made the profit itself on those shares because it had not the means of making the investment. The directors were in a fiduciary relationship to Regal and were not allowed to benefit from this position. Lord Russell said: 'I am of opinion that the directors standing in a fiduciary relationship to Regal in regard to the exercise of their powers as directors, and having obtained these shares by reason and only by reason of the fact that they were directors of Regal and in the course of the execution of that office, are accountable for the profits which they have made out of them.'

Cook v Deeks (1916) PC

The Toronto Construction Co (Toronto) had been successful in obtaining a number of contracts from the Canadian Pacific Railway Co (CPR). Toronto had four shareholders, who also constituted its board of directors. Three of the directors fell out with the fourth, Cook, and when the three learnt of a new CPR contract available for tender they negotiated for it in the name of Toronto and then formed a new company to take it, so as to exclude Cook. A resolution was subsequently passed by Toronto declaring that Toronto claimed no interest in the CPR contract. Cook claimed that the benefit of the contract properly belonged to Toronto.

Held The Privy Council held that the new company and its three directors must account for the profit made. The contract was gained by the three whilst in their positions as fiduciaries within Toronto. The benefit of the contract thus belonged in equity to Toronto and the three directors could not use their voting power to vest it in themselves. The court noted that this would amount to 'forfeiting the interests and the property of the minority of shareholders in favour of the majority' which could not be sanctioned by the court.

Industrial Development Consultants Ltd v Cooley (1972)

The defendant was the managing director of the plaintiff company and had formerly been an architect with the West Midlands Gas Board. He entered into negotiations on behalf of the company with the Eastern Gas Board. Eastern Gas informed the defendant that it would enter into the contract with him personally but not with the company. The defendant resigned as managing director of the company (on the pretext of ill-health) in order to take up the Gas Board contract. The company sued for the profit made.

Held The defendant was liable for all benefits accruing under the contract, even though the plaintiff company had lost no corporate opportunity. Whilst managing director of the plaintiff company, a fiduciary relationship existed between himself and the company, and he was therefore under a duty to disclose all information revealed to him in the course of his dealings with the Gas Board. The defendant's actions had put his personal interest in direct conflict with the interests of the company, and this constituted a breach of his fiduciary duty for which he was accountable.

Movitex Ltd v Bulfield (1986)

The plaintiff company contracted to buy a freehold property that it needed as business premises. The defendants, B and P, were directors of the company. The company was unable to complete the purchase due to insufficient finance, whereupon B, on behalf of the company, arranged for the property to be conveyed to CRS, a company set up by B and P. CRS paid the purchase price and granted leases of the property to the company. The company sought to have the purchase and the leases set aside on the ground that B and P, as directors of the company, had breached their fiduciary duties under the no-conflict rule.

Held The transactions would not be set aside. The no-conflict rule imposed a disability on the directors not a duty, the consequence of which was that transactions would be voidable by the company. The rule could thus be modified by the company's articles as this did not involve exempting directors from liability for breach of duty. Under the articles, directors were under a duty to disclose full information as to the type and extent of their interests. On the facts B and P had fulfilled this duty.

Neptune (Vehicle Washing Equipment) Ltd v Fitzgerald (1995)

This case raised the question of the meaning of disclosure of a director's interest in accordance with s 317 of the Companies Act (CA) 1985 where that director is the sole director of the company concerned. The defendant was the sole director of the plaintiff company. The company's articles contained a provision that any director of the company must disclose his interest in a contract or arrangement with the company at a meeting of the directors pursuant to s 317 of the CA 1985. The defendant, at a meeting at which he and the company's secretary were present, passed resolutions terminating his employment with the company and paying him over £100,000 in severance pay due under his employment contract. The minutes of the meeting did not record any specific declaration by him of his interest in these resolutions. The company successfully applied for summary judgment that the defendant was in breach of his fiduciary duty in passing these resolutions and that they constituted unlawful self dealing. The defendant appealed to the High Court from this finding on summary judgment, arguing that he had an arguable defence on the substantive issue of breach of fiduciary duty and the matter should be allowed to proceed to trial.

Held The appeal was successful but Mr Justice Lightman made some interesting points about the meaning of the obligation in s 317 of the CA 1985 in a company where there is only one director. There could be a valid board meeting with only one director in attendance but even then the disclosure of any interest in the business of the meeting by that director should be recorded in the minutes of the meeting, although it need not be made out loud. However, where, as here, there was another person, usually the company secretary in attendance, then the disclosure must be made out loud in the hearing of those present, as well as being recorded in the minutes in order for it to be in compliance with s 317 of the CA 1985.

Bhullar v Bhullar 2003 EWCA Civ 424

7   Shareholders' meetings

7.1   Requisitioning a meeting

Baillie v Oriental Telephone & Electric Co (1915)

The directors of the respondent company passed resolutions altering the articles of association of one of the company's subsidiary companies (of which they were the directors also), increasing their fixed remuneration and giving them a percentage of the net profits. It was drawn to their attention that this should be sanctioned by the shareholders at a general meeting of the company. An extraordinary general meeting was convened by the directors for the purpose of ratifying the original resolutions by special resolution. The notice convening the meeting was accompanied by a circular, with the notice setting out the proposed resolutions. Neither document gave particulars as to the very large amount of remuneration which had been received by the directors. The resolutions were passed. The action was brought by a shareholder.

Held The Court of Appeal decided that the notice failed to give a sufficiently full and frank disclosure of the resolutions upon which the shareholders were being asked to vote. The resolutions were declared invalid and not binding upon the company.

Tiessen v Henderson (1899)

The plaintiffs were shareholders in a mining company, of which the defendants were directors. The company was about to undergo a reconstruction. Various proposals were laid before two extraordinary general meetings, which were detailed in the notices for the meetings. However, the defendants failed to disclose their pecuniary interests in their favoured proposal.

Held The plaintiffs obtained an order invalidating the relevant resolution. The notice of an extraordinary general meeting must disclose all material facts to enable each shareholder to determine whether or not to attend the meeting. The fact that a director has a pecuniary interest in a proposed transaction is a material fact.

7.2 Proxies

Cousins v International Brick Co Ltd (1931) CA

The plaintiff originally secured proxies representing the votes of a number of shareholders in the defendant company. These were intended to be used in a vote to secure the election of Mr C as a director of the company. At the meeting at which the proxies were to be counted, a number of those who had originally given their proxies to the plaintiff attended and were allowed to vote against Mr C, although their proxies had not been validly revoked. Mr C was defeated and the plaintiff brought an action claiming that the proxies had been wrongfully disallowed.

Held Where a proxy had not been validly revoked, the shareholder was free to attend the meeting and vote personally, and that this allowed the vote tendered by proxy to be properly rejected.

Re the British Union for the Abolition of Vivisection (1995)

The company (BUAV) was a company limited by guarantee which did not allow voting by proxy at meetings, but instead demanded attendance in order to vote. After a long and confrontational annual general meeting an extraordinary meeting was convened at which one of the resolutions was to introduce voting by proxy. The meeting had to be closed by the police for fear of a breach of the peace after it degenerated into a disorderly tumult. The executive committee (board of directors) of BUAV applied to the court (under s 371 of the Companies Act 1985) to convene a meeting to vote on a special resolution to alter the company's articles to introduce voting by proxy. The applicants sought to restrict attendance to the executive committee and to allow all other votes to be cast by way of a postal ballot, thus dispensing with the requirement of personal attendance in accordance with the articles.

Held The court made the order. It was clear on the facts that to comply with the requirements in the company's constitution was impracticable in the circumstances due to the conduct of some of the members at previous meetings. Accordingly, a meeting would be ordered as requested by the executive committee at which postal votes would be allowed.

7.3 Resolutions

Parker & Cooper Ltd v Reading (1926)

The plaintiff company issued a debenture to the defendant as security for a loan. The articles of the company prescribed that the instrument be signed by the directors and sealed in their presence. The signatures were duly attached but the instrument was not sealed in their presence. The four shareholders of the company had discussed the transaction and assented to it individually, but no general meeting had been held. The company's liquidator disputed the validity of the debenture and the resolution.

Held The court held the debenture and the resolution authorising its issue to be valid. In the course of his judgment, Astbury J stated: 'where the transaction is *intra vires* and honest, and especially if it is for the benefit of the company, it cannot be upset if the assent of all the corporators is given to it. I do not think it matters in the least whether that assent is given at different times or simultaneously'. Thus valid assent was given to the irregular transactions.

Re Duomatic Ltd (1969)

For a period of 15 months, the two directors of the company were its only ordinary shareholders. Under the articles of the company, remuneration of directors had to be determined from time to time by resolution of the company in general meeting. No such resolutions were passed but the two directors drew sums according to their needs and entered them into the accounts as 'directors' salaries'. The liquidator of the company sought to recover these sums from the two directors.

Held Although none of the payments were authorised by resolution, the clear assent of all the ordinary shareholders was as binding as a resolution and the payments could not be disturbed. Buckley J said: 'where it can be shown that all the shareholders who have a right to attend and vote at a general meeting of the company assent to some matter which a general meeting of the company could carry into effect, that assent is as binding as a resolution in general meeting would be'.

Cane v Jones (1980)

Two brothers, H and P, formed a company and were the sole directors of that company. The shareholding of the company was divided equally between members of H's family and members of P's family. The company's articles provided for the election of a chairman by the directors, who should have a casting vote at board meetings and should preside over and have a casting vote at general meetings of the company. An agreement was made between all the shareholders that the chairman should cease to be entitled to use his casting vote. The management of the company became deadlocked. The plaintiff claimed the informal agreement was effective to alter the company's articles, and thus the defendants could not exercise a casting vote.

Held Despite the lack of a meeting or a resolution in writing to comply with the statutory requirements regarding the alteration of a company's articles, the agreement was effective. The agreement represented the unanimous will of the shareholders acting together and had the same effect as would a special resolution altering the company's articles so as to deprive the chairman of his casting vote.

7.4 Role of chairman

John v Rees (1969)

The plaintiff was the president and chairman of the Pembrokeshire Divisional Labour Party. At a properly constituted meeting, a conflict of views arose and there was evidence of noise, disorder and some minor violence. The plaintiff, as chairman, warned that it would be impossible to continue the meeting if the disorder persisted. Upon the continuance of the disorder, the chairman announced the adjournment of the meeting and left, accompanied by a number of others. The meeting continued without the chairman and new officers were elected. The plaintiff sought an order invalidating these actions.

Held The chairman possessed an inherent power to adjourn a meeting in the event of disorder if he acted *bona fide* and if the adjournment were for no longer than necessary for the restoration of order. However, in the present case, the disorder was not sufficient to warrant an adjournment. The meeting remained in being and the elections of the new officers were thus valid.

National Dwellings Society v Sykes (1894)

At the plaintiff company's annual general meeting, the chair was taken by the defendant. The chairman moved the first resolution, to which an amendment was moved by shareholders. The chairman ruled this amendment out and proceeded with the original resolution, which was defeated on a show of hands. Upon this, the chairman said: 'I declare the resolution to be lost, and I dissolve the meeting', although much of the business of the meeting had not been disposed of. The shareholders elected another member to be chairman and continued the meeting, passing certain resolutions, and then adjourning it to a later date. The legality of the defendant's conduct was challenged.

Held The duty of a chairman is to preserve order, to take care that the proceedings are conducted in a proper manner, and that the sense of the meeting is properly ascertained regarding any question which is properly before the meeting. The chairman has no power to stop or adjourn a meeting at his own will, and if he purports to do so then the meeting may resolve to continue with the business for which it was convened, and to appoint another chairman for that purpose.

Byng v London Life Association Ltd (1990) CA

An extraordinary general meeting of the company had been summoned for 12 noon at a London cinema, in order for a vote to be taken on a specific matter. Expecting a large attendance, audio-visual links were set up in other rooms in the building. These audio-visual links failed to function. The cinema held 300, but 800 members turned up. Without following the procedure laid out in the articles of the company the chairman adjourned the meeting to a larger venue that same afternoon. Only 600 people could attend this adjourned meeting, and there was no time to arrange proxies for those who could not attend. At the afternoon meeting a resolution was passed. The plaintiff sought declarations that the purported meetings and resolution were invalid. The action was dismissed and the plaintiff appealed.

Held The Court of Appeal held that although a motion to adjourn could not be put to the meeting, the chairman had a common law power to adjourn the meeting in such circumstances. However, the appeal was allowed. Although the chairman had acted in good faith, he was under a duty to act reasonably to facilitate the limited purpose for which the power to adjourn existed. The chairman failed to take into account all the relevant factors, ie the urgency of passing the resolution; that members unable to attend the afternoon meeting had no time to arrange proxies; and that consideration should have been given to abandoning the meeting. The decision of the chairman to adjourn the meeting was therefore invalid.

7.5 Quorum

Sharp v Dawes (1876)

A meeting of a Cornish mining company was convened. The only persons to attend were the secretary of the company (the plaintiff, who was not a member) and one shareholder, who took the chair and conducted the business of the meeting. One of the purposes for which the meeting was summoned was to make a call, and this was passed by resolution. The call was made on the defendant, who refused to pay it.

Held The Court of Appeal decided that the meeting was a nullity and thus the call was invalid. A single shareholder could not constitute a meeting. In the course of his judgment, Mellish LJ stated: 'It is clear that, according to the ordinary use of the English language, a meeting could no more be constituted by one person than a meeting could have been constituted if no shareholder at all had attended.'

Re London Flats Ltd (1969)

The company went into a members' voluntary liquidation. The first liquidator died within a month and the applicant called an extraordinary general meeting of the company for the purpose of filling the vacant position of liquidator. The applicant and the respondent were the only persons entitled to attend and vote as members. The respondent declared himself to be chairman and, after allowing the applicant to propose that L be appointed liquidator of the company, proposed an amendment that he (the respondent) would propose himself as liquidator. The applicant left the room before the respondent could do so. The amendment was carried by one vote in favour to none against. The question arose as to the validity of the respondent's appointment.

Held The respondent's purported appointment of himself as liquidator was a nullity. At the time when he was proposing himself as such the applicant had left the meeting. This leaving only one member present there was, therefore, no meeting as a single shareholder could not constitute a meeting.

East v Bennett Bros (1911)

The constitution of a company provided that no new shares ranking equally or in priority to the preference shares should be issued unless sanctioned by an extraordinary resolution of the holders of preference shares at a separate 'meeting' of the preference shareholders. The company resolved to increase its capital by issuing further preference shares. B was the holder of all the original preference shares. He was thus the only member present at the class 'meeting' at which he resolved to sanction the new preference share issue. The validity of the meeting and the share issue was questioned.

Held Because of the fact that there was nothing in the company's constitution to prevent the whole of the preference shares being held by one shareholder, the word 'meeting' in the constitution must be taken in the circumstances to be applicable to the case of a single shareholder. Therefore, the company's constitution had been complied with and the new preference shares validly issued.

Re El Sombrero Ltd (1958)

The applicant held 90% of the company's shares, the other 10% being split equally between the two directors of the company. Under the company's constitution, the quorum for general meetings was two members present in person or by proxy. No general meeting had ever been held and the applicant had been unsuccessful in his attempts to force the directors, as the only other shareholders, to attend two extraordinary general meetings. The purpose of the meetings was to pass resolutions removing the two directors and replacing them with two other persons. The applicant applied to the court (under s 135 of the Companies Act 1948) asking for a meeting to be called and a direction that one shareholder should be deemed sufficient to constitute a quorum at such a meeting. The directors opposed the application.

Held The application was granted. The desired meeting of the company could not, in all practical senses, be conducted in accordance with the company's constitution and the court was prepared to use its statutory discretion to order a meeting to be held despite shareholder opposition. The court would order that one member alone would constitute a quorum at the meeting because otherwise the applicant would be deprived of his statutory right to remove the directors by ordinary resolution, and the directors had themselves failed to perform their statutory duty to call an annual general meeting in the knowledge that it would lead to their removal.

8 Minority shareholders

8.1 The rule in *Foss v Harbottle*

Foss v Harbottle (1843)
The two plaintiffs, suing 'on behalf of themselves and all the other members of the corporation, except those who committed the injuries complained of' alleged that the defendants, who were the directors and promoters of the company, had, *inter alia*, sold land to the company at an undisclosed profit.

Held The individual minority shareholders were not the proper plaintiffs and could not therefore sue. If a wrong had been committed it had been committed against the company and therefore the proper plaintiff was the company. It was not open to individual members to assume to themselves the right of suing in the name of the company. Although this was a rule which could be departed from, it should not be, save for 'reasons of a very urgent character'. In the circumstances, there was nothing to prevent the company from obtaining redress in its corporate character regarding the matters complained of.

8.1.1 Special majority

Edwards v Halliwell (1950) CA
The constitution of the defendant trade union provided that contributions were not to be altered without a ballot of the membership at which a two-thirds majority had been obtained. A resolution was passed by a general meeting of delegates increasing the contributions of members, although no ballot was taken. The two plaintiffs, as members of the union, sued the union and two members of its executive committee for a declaration that the resolution was invalid.

Held The plaintiffs succeeded. The act in question violated a requirement in the articles for a special majority. Jenkins LJ summarised the rule in *Foss v Harbottle*:

> First, the proper plaintiff in an action in respect of any wrong alleged to be done to a company or association of persons is *prima facie* the company or association of persons itself. Secondly, where the alleged wrong is a transaction which might be made binding on the company or association and on all its members

by a simple majority of the members, no individual member of the company is allowed to maintain an action in respect of that matter for the simple reason that, if a mere majority of the members of the company or association is in favour of what has been done, then *cadet quaestio*.

8.1.2 Shareholder can bring action to enforce personal rights

Pender v Lushington (1877) CA

The articles of a company entitled every member to one vote for each 10 shares held, up to a maximum of 100 votes. The plaintiff had registered his shareholding in the names of several nominees in order to exceed this voting limit. At a general meeting of the company, the chairman refused to accept the votes of the nominees and rejected them as invalid. The plaintiff brought an action against the directors, naming the company as co-plaintiff, on behalf of himself, the shareholders and the company.

Held The act complained of was an invasion of the personal rights of a member and the court thus accepted the plaintiff's claim. Jessel MR stated that the action could be brought either in the company's name by the minority shareholder or alternatively in the minority shareholder's name. On the latter alternative, Jessel MR said: 'This is an action by Mr Pender for himself. He is a member of the company, and whether he votes with the majority or the minority, he is entitled to have his vote recorded – an individual right in respect of which he has a right to sue.'

Wood v Odessa Waterworks (1889)

The articles of the waterworks company empowered the directors, with the sanction of the company, to declare a dividend 'to be paid' to the members. The directors instead recommended that members should be given debenture-bonds bearing interest, and redeemable at par, by annual drawings, extending over 30 years. This recommendation was approved by an ordinary resolution of the company in general meeting. The plaintiff sought an injunction restraining the company from acting on the resolution on the ground that it breached the articles.

Held The injunction was granted. The resolution of the general meeting was not in accordance with the articles of the company and the directors must be restrained from acting thereon. The plaintiff, as a shareholder of the company, was able to enforce his personal right to a dividend paid in cash, rather than as proposed, as laid down in the company's articles.

8.1.3 Fraud by wrongdoers in control

Cook v Deeks (1916) PC

The Toronto Construction Co (Toronto) had been successful in obtaining a number of contracts from the Canadian Pacific Railway Co (CPR). Toronto had four shareholders, who also constituted its board of directors. Three of the directors fell out with the fourth, Cook, and when the three learnt of a new CPR contract available for tender they negotiated for it in the name of Toronto and then formed a new company to take it, so as to exclude Cook. A resolution was subsequently passed by Toronto declaring that Toronto claimed no interest in the CPR contract. Cook claimed that the benefit of the contract properly belonged to Toronto.

Held The Privy Council held that the new company and its three directors must account for the profit made. The contract was gained by the three whilst in their positions as fiduciaries within Toronto. The benefit of the contract thus belonged in equity to Toronto and the three directors could not use their voting power to vest it in themselves. The court noted that this would amount to 'forfeiting the interests and the property of the minority of shareholders in favour of the majority' which could not be sanctioned by the court.

Daniels v Daniels (1978)

The plaintiffs were minority shareholders in the company. The first and second defendants, Mr and Mrs Daniels, were majority shareholders and directors. The plaintiffs alleged that the defendants had caused the selling of certain company land to Mrs Daniels at an undervalue. It was sold to Mrs Daniels for £4,250 and she sold it four years later for £120,000. The defendants applied for the action to be struck out as disclosing no reasonable cause of action.

Held The application to strike out the action was dismissed. The minority shareholders were entitled to bring an action where the majority of directors had benefitted themselves at the expense of the company, even though this was through negligence and without fraud. Templeman J stated: '[A] minority shareholder who has no other remedy may sue where directors use their powers intentionally or unintentionally, fraudulently or negligently in a manner which benefits themselves at the expense of the company.'

Pavlides v Jensen (1956)

The defendant company, Tunnel Asbestos Cement Co Ltd, were alleged to have sold an asbestos mine in Cyprus at a gross undervalue. The mine was sold to Cyprus Asbestos Mines Ltd, in which the defendant company held 25% of the issued share capital, at a price of £182,000. The plaintiff claimed that it was worth in the region of £1,000,000. The sale was carried through by the defendant directors and was not submitted to the approval of the defendant company in general meeting. The plaintiff, a minority shareholder, brought an action on behalf of himself and all the other shareholders in the company except the three defendant directors, alleging gross negligence. The plaintiff claimed the entitlement to bring the action on two grounds. First, that the company's articles prevented him from requisitioning or attending a general meeting of the company, and secondly, that the defendant directors were in a position to control the company and so prevent the company taking any action against them.

Held The court held that mere negligence was not a fraud on the minority and that it was open to the company in general meeting to decide not to sue – mere negligence could be ratified by resolution whereas fraud could not. The action was struck out.

Prudential Assurance Co Ltd v Newman Industries Ltd (No 2) (1982) CA

The plaintiff was an institutional investor which held a minority shareholding in Newman, the first defendant. The plaintiff company sought to bring a derivative action against two directors of the defendant company alleging that they had defrauded the company of over £440,000. The transaction by the directors which was the cause of the allegations had been approved by the company in general meeting. The two directors were not majority shareholders. The plaintiff claimed that the shareholders had been misled into approving the actions of the directors.

Held The Court of Appeal decided that the general rule was that it was the company that should, *prima facie*, bring the action and therefore not a minority shareholder, where there were allegations of fraud. It was only in circumstances where the board of directors of the company was under the control of the alleged fraudsters that a derivative action should be brought. The question of control of the board was a preliminary question to be determined before a derivative action should be heard. On the question of control, the court said it embraced 'a broad spectrum extending from an overall absolute majority of votes at one end to a majority of votes at the other end made up of those likely to be cast by the delinquent himself plus those voting with him as a result of influence or apathy'.

Estmanco (Kilner House) Ltd v GLC (1982)

The Greater London Council formed the Estmanco company to manage a block of 60 council-owned flats. The council entered into an agreement with the company to sell off the flats to owner-occupiers. The company had 60 shares, one of which was transferred from the council to the buyer upon each sale of a flat, the voting right being retained until all the flats had been sold. Control of the council changed after the sale of 12 flats and a new housing policy adopted not to sell off the remaining flats. An action against the council was brought by two directors for breach of contract, but the council as majority shareholder and with voting control resolved in general meeting to discontinue the action. One of the 12 flat owners, as a member of the company, sought leave to bring a derivative action on behalf of the company.

Held The minority shareholder's application was granted. Megarry VC held that whatever 'fraud on the minority' meant it was 'wide enough to cover the present case' and if not 'should now be made wide enough'. Fraud on the minority therefore included the abuse or misuse of power by the majority, in this case voting power. Although the council as majority shareholders owed no fiduciary duty to the company and could vote in its own interest, this did not confer an unrestricted right to pass a resolution depriving the minority of rights simply because it thought this to be in the best interests of the company.

Smith v Croft (No 2) (1987)

The plaintiffs alleged various improprieties against the company for which it would be entitled to relief. The plaintiffs and their supporters held around 14% of the voting rights, with the defendant majority shareholders holding 63%. W Ltd, a company not under the control of either party, held 20% of the voting rights and opposed the continuance of the action. The defendants brought a motion to strike out the action.

Held Although a minority shareholder may have *locus standi* to bring an action, it did not follow that the minority shareholder had an indefeasible right to prosecute the action on the company's behalf. In such a case, the views of the independent shareholders had to be taken into account. Their votes would be disregarded only if the court was satisfied that they would be cast in favour of either party rather than for the benefit of the company, or if there was a substantial risk of that being the case. The evidence was that the majority of independent shareholders were genuinely not in favour of continuing the action and thus the action of the minority shareholder would be struck out.

Barrett and Duckett & Others (1994) CA

The plaintiff was a 50% shareholder in Nightingale Travel Ltd. The first defendant was the sole director and other shareholder of the company. The plaintiff brought proceedings on behalf of the company alleging, *inter alia*, that the defendants had set up another company and had diverted the company's legitimate business to that new company. The first defendant had presented a petition to wind up Nightingale Travel. The defendants sought to strike out the derivative action.

Held The Court of Appeal struck out the action. A derivative action would be allowed to be brought by a shareholder if brought *bona fide* for the benefit of the company for wrongs done to the company where no other remedy would lie. The winding up petition provided an adequate alternative remedy to the derivative action. Additionally, there was an element of personal interest in the plaintiff's action which was not associated with the *bona fide* interests of the company

Wallersteiner v Moir (No 2) (1975) CA

The case arose out of an ongoing legal battle between Mr Moir and Dr Wallersteiner. Wallersteiner was managing director and majority shareholder (holding 80% of the shares) of Hartley Baird Ltd. On behalf of the company, Moir brought a derivative action as a minority shareholder, claiming that Wallersteiner had achieved his 80% majority by a cheat, having 'not paid a penny in hard cash' for the shares (in the words of Lord Denning MR). The present case was an application by Moir for financial assistance to carry on the action.

Held The Court of Appeal held that where in good faith and on reasonable grounds a minority shareholder has brought an action on behalf of the company, and where the benefit of the action if successful will accrue to the company and only indirectly therefore to the plaintiff (as a member), the court may order the company to pay the plaintiff's costs. It must have been reasonable for an independent board of directors to have brought the action in the company name.

8.2   'Just and equitable' winding up: s 122(1)(g) of the Insolvency Act 1986

Ebrahimi v Westbourne Galleries (1973) HL

Ebrahami and Nazar ran a successful carpet business as a partnership which they went on to incorporate. Nazar's son George was brought into the business and shares transferred to him. Friction occurred and Nazar and George excluded Ebrahami from the business, removing him as a director. The profits of the business were paid out in the form of directors' salaries and not in dividends. Due to his exclusion, Ebrahami saw none of the profits. He therefore petitioned for the company to be wound up on 'just and equitable' grounds.

Held The House of Lords unanimously granted the order for the company to be wound up. Lord Wilberforce defined the concept of 'just and equitable' as:

> a recognition of the fact that a limited company is more than a mere legal entity, with a personality in law of its own; that ... there are individuals, with rights, expectations and obligations *inter se* which are not necessarily submerged in the company structure. ... It does, as equity always does, enable the court to subject the exercise of legal rights to equitable considerations, that is, of personal character arising between one individual and another, which may make it unjust or inequitable, to insist on legal rights, or to exercise them in a particular way.

His Lordship proceeded to set out some of the situations which he had in mind:

> The superimposition of equitable considerations requires something more, which typically may include one, or probably more, of the following elements: (i) an association formed or continued on the basis of a personal relationship, involving mutual confidence ... (ii) an agreement, or understanding, that all, or

some (for there may be 'sleeping' members), of the shareholders shall participate in the conduct of the business; (iii) restriction upon the transfer of the members' interest in the company – so that if confidence is lost, or one member is removed from management, he cannot take out his stake and go elsewhere.

8.2.1 Circumstances in which petitions have succeeded

Re Yenidje Tobacco Co Ltd (1916) CA

The company had two shareholders who were each directors and held an equal number of the shares in the company. The company was incorporated as the result of an amalgamation of two separate businesses. Due to continued disagreement between the two, there was effectively a total deadlock in the management of the affairs of the company. The parties were so hostile towards one another that neither of them would speak to the other. A petition was presented alleging that a complete deadlock had arisen, that the substratum of the company was gone, and that it was 'just and equitable' for a winding up order to be made.

Held The Court of Appeal decided that it was 'just and equitable' that the company should be wound up. There were clearly grounds for dissolution if it were a case of partnership, and the same principle would be applied in the instant case where there was in essence a partnership in the guise of a company.

Re Cuthbert Cooper & Sons Ltd (1937)

The articles of association of a family company stated that the directors might in their absolute discretion refuse to register any transfer of shares without assigning any reason for such refusal. This power extended to the registration of the executors of a deceased shareholder. On the death of a shareholder the directors refused to register the executors of the deceased in their capacity of beneficiaries under the deceased's will as members of the company. The executors presented a petition for the winding up of the company on just and equitable grounds.

Held The court refused to make a winding up order. Although the company resembled a partnership and the principles applicable to a partnership were therefore applied to the company, there were no grounds on which it would be 'just and equitable' to have the company wound up.

Re A & BC Chewing Gum Ltd (1975)

The petitioners purchased one-third of the shareholding in the company on the basis of a shareholders' agreement that although they were minority shareholders they should have equal control with the respondents, the Coakleys, who were brothers and directors of the company and who owned the remaining two-thirds of the shares. The company experienced financial problems. The petitioners appointed one of the respondent brothers as their director and representative. Due to dissatisfaction with him, the respondent brother was eventually removed as the petitioners' director and a third party appointed in his place. The respondents refused to recognise this, due to an alleged agreement between the parties that the respondent brother would not be removed. The petitioners applied for an order that the company be wound up on the ground that it would be just and equitable to do so.

Held The court found no binding agreement between the parties to rescind the petitioners' right to nominate a director. The respondents had therefore denied a right held by the petitioners which had been established by the company's articles and the shareholders' agreement. The repudiation of such a fundamental right by the respondents amounted to grounds for the company to be wound up on just and equitable grounds.

Loch v John Blackwood Ltd (1924) PC

A company was registered with the purpose of carrying on the testator's business and dividing between members of a family the profits thereof as laid down by the testator's will. The directors failed to hold general meetings, submit accounts, or recommend a dividend, laying themselves open to the suspicion that their reason for so doing was to keep the minority in ignorance of the company's standing in order to acquire their shares at an undervalue. A petition was presented by the minority to have the company wound up on the ground that it would be just and equitable to do so.

Held Due to the domestic nature of the company, the Privy Council held that in the circumstances it would be just and equitable for the company to be wound up. There had been proved on the facts a loss of confidence in the probity of the directors. In the words of Lord Shaw: '[W]henever the lack of confidence is rested on a lack of probity in the conduct of the company's affairs, then the former is justified by the latter and it is, under the statute, just and equitable that the company be wound up.'

Re Bleriot Manufacturing Aircraft Co (1916)

The company was incorporated to manufacture, buy, sell and deal in aircraft. The prospectus of the company stated that it was the object of the company to acquire and extend the Bleriot aircraft business. The company failed to acquire the Bleriot aircraft business and had no future prospect of so doing. A petition for winding up the company was presented which detailed this failure. The petition also alleged that control of the business had been improperly taken by two men, Lawson and Swinburn. There were also allegations that various statutory requirements had not been complied with. For these reasons, the petitioner said that the substratum of the company was gone and it was just and equitable to grant an order winding up the company.

Held The order was granted. The company had been formed specifically for the Bleriot business to be acquired and therefore the substratum of the company had been lost. This was sufficient ground to wind up the company on just and equitable grounds. Additionally, Neville J proceeded to state that there was another ground. The misconduct of the directors was also sufficient for a winding up on just and equitable grounds.

Re Zinotty Properties Ltd (1984)

A and B formed a company to acquire and develop a particular site. Two shares were held by the petitioner, which was controlled by A, and six shares were held by X Ltd, controlled by B and C. A assumed that he would be appointed a director of the company, but instead B and C were appointed to the exclusion of A. On completion of the project, B and C began to use the company to acquire further sites. A was not consulted. The petitioner presented a petition for the compulsory winding up of the company on the ground that it would be just and equitable to do so, submitting that the mutual trust and confidence between the parties had broken down.

Held Although the affairs of the individuals were conducted through other companies, the company itself had been established on a basis of trust and confidence between them. The court held that this mutual trust and confidence had broken down, as evidenced by the facts, and that it would be just and equitable to grant a compulsory winding up order.

8.2.2   Availability of other remedies: s 125(2) of the Insolvency Act 1986

Virdi v Abbey Leisure Ltd (1989) CA

A company was formed for the express purpose of purchasing, refurbishing and then selling a night club. This having been achieved a dispute arose as to the future of the company, whose only assets were the proceeds from the sale. The petitioner, a holder of 40% of the company's equity, applied to have the company wound up on the ground that it would be just and equitable to do so, in order to realise his 40% of the proceeds of sale. It was accepted that he had a right to an order unless he had another remedy which it would not be unreasonable for him to use. Hoffman J struck out the petition as the petitioner had the alternative remedy of accepting an offer to buy his shares at a price determined by an accountant, a provision contained in the articles of the company, and was acting unreasonably by not so doing.

Held The Court of Appeal reversed the decision of the court at first instance and granted an order to wind up the company on the just and equitable ground. It was not unreasonable for the petitioner to seek a winding up order rather than use the alternative method of realising his share of the sale proceeds through the provision in the articles. There was a risk that a valuation would undervalue the shares of a minority shareholder and there was nothing unreasonable in the petitioner refusing to accept that risk.

8.3 Unfair prejudice: s 459 of the Companies Act 1985

8.3.1 The old law

Re H R Harmer Ltd (1959)

Mr Harmer, the founder of the company, made a gift to his sons of the majority of shares in the company but retained voting control in general meeting. He continued to run the business as if it were solely his, disregarding resolutions of the board of directors, assuming powers he did not possess and ignoring the wishes of his sons, who were directors as well as shareholders. It became impossible to run the business successfully. At first instance Roxburgh J held that a case of oppression had been made out (under s 210 of the Companies Act (CA) 1948). Mr Harmer was ordered not to interfere with the affairs of the company otherwise than in accordance with decisions of the board of directors. He was appointed as president of the company for life, but the office was devoid of any duties, rights or powers. Mr Harmer appealed.

Held The Court of Appeal dismissed the appeal. The affairs of the company had been conducted in a manner oppressive to the sons as members. The sons were therefore entitled to relief under s 210 as requested. Oppression was not limited to such as was designed to obtain pecuniary advantage.

Scottish Co-operative Wholesale Society v Meyer (1959) HL

The Scottish Co-operative Wholesale Society formed a subsidiary company to manufacture rayon material, because it could not obtain a licence to do so without the experience of the petitioners, Meyer and Lucas, minority shareholders and directors of the subsidiary. Scottish Co-operative owned the majority of shares and appointed three directors as nominees on the board of the subsidiary. When the licensing requirement was lifted, Scottish Co-operative decided to transfer the business to one of its own departments. The nominee directors participated with Scottish Co-operative although the transfer was not in the company's best interests. The business of the subsidiary company having been transferred, it came to an almost complete standstill with a corresponding drop in its share price. The petitioners sought an order, on the ground of oppression under s 210 of the CA 1948, for the purchase of their shares at their original value.

Held The House of Lords decided that the conduct of Scottish Co-operative had been oppressive within the meaning of s 210. This amounted to conduct of the affairs of the subsidiary company as it was effected through the nominee directors, the transactions of the two being inseparable. The original petitioners were entitled to the relief sought as the purchase of their shares by Scottish Co-operative would effect a cessation in the oppression.

8.3.2 What is 'unfair prejudice'?

Re Bovey Hotel Ventures Ltd (1981)

In 1963, a husband and wife formed a company called Bovey Hotel Ventures Ltd and appointed themselves the directors and equal joint shareholders thereof. It was a restaurant business. The couple separated in 1971 and afterwards the strife between the two meant there were difficulties in running the company. The husband ran the business and excluded the wife from it. She suspected him of taking funds out of the business for his own purpose and when this came to the attention of the Inland Revenue he was found to have done so. There was also an investigation by the Commissioners of Customs and Excise into VAT irregularities on the sale of wines and spirits. It was found that the company owed £3,100 in back duty for VAT purposes, representing a disappearance from the company cellars of wines and spirits worth around £26,600. These matters led the wife to believe that she was being treated unfairly, and she presented a petition under s 75 of the CA 1980.

Held The actions of the husband were unfairly prejudicial to the wife as a shareholder of the company and she would be granted the relief she sought. In the course of his judgment Slade J said:

> [A] member of a company will be able to bring himself within the section if he can show that the value of his shareholding in the company has been seriously diminished or at least seriously jeopardised by reason of a course of conduct on the part of those persons who have *de facto* control of the company, which has been unfair to the member concerned. The test of unfairness must, I think, be an objective, not a subjective, one. In other words, it is not necessary for the petitioner to show that the persons who have *de facto* control of the company have acted as they did in the conscious knowledge that this was unfair to the petitioner or that they were acting in bad faith; the test, I think, is whether a reasonable bystander observing the consequences of their conduct, would regard it as having unfairly prejudiced the petitioner's interests.

Re R A Noble & Sons (Clothing) Ltd (1983)

The company was incorporated by Noble and Bailey. It was agreed that Bailey would introduce £10,000 into the venture and both would hold 50 shares. Bailey also had to renovate a shop for the company and Noble would look after the company's affairs for a salary. Bailey's £10,000 contribution was made through a company known as Anafield Builders Ltd. A dispute arose which led to disagreement between Bailey and Noble as to the management and organisation of the company's affairs. Contact between the two became infrequent and eventually Bailey wrote to Noble wishing to sever his connections, and claiming repayment of the loan made by Anafield Builders. Anafield presented a petition under s 75 of the CA 1980 alleging that neither Anafield nor Bailey had been informed of, or adequately consulted on, important transactions affecting the company and that Noble had improperly assumed control of the company and excluded Bailey from involvement in its affairs.

Held The treatment of Anafield was not unfairly prejudicial within the terms of s 75 and thus the relief sought would not be granted. Anafield's exclusion from participation in the business of the company was largely attributable to Bailey's disinterest and Noble's wish to get on with the affairs of management. Noble was not in any way guilty of underhand conduct. Nourse J relied on the dictum of Slade J in *Re Bovey Hotel Ventures Ltd* in reaching his decision (see above, p 79).

Re A Company (No 00477 of 1986)

The petitioners were the sole shareholders of A Ltd. They sold these shares to O plc in return for an issue of shares in O plc on the understanding that the relationship between themselves and the controllers of O plc would be that of a 'partnership'. The petition was brought after the dismissal of one of the petitioners (Mr S) in breach of his service contract with O plc. The petition alleged that the dismissal was contrary to the 'partnership' agreement and unfairly prejudicial, and also that the conduct of the controllers had affected the value of the petitioners' shares in O plc. The respondents argued that the allegations did not affect them as members of O plc but instead concerned Mr S as an employee and themselves as vendors of shares. The respondents applied to strike out the petition.

Held The motion to strike out the petition was dismissed. The principle underlying s 459 of the CA 1985 was that the court had jurisdiction to grant relief on a finding of conduct which was unfairly prejudicial to the interests of the members *qua* members and not in any other capacity. However, the interests of the members were not necessarily limited to the strict legal rights given under the constitution of the company. The use of the word 'unfairly' allowed the court to consider wider equitable considerations.

Re London School of Electronics Ltd (1986)

The company (LSE) ran courses in electronics. The petitioner in the matter was a director and 25% shareholder of the company. The remaining shares were held by the respondent company, City Tutorial College Ltd (CTC), which was substantially owned by A and G. CTC employed the petitioner as a teacher until relationships broke down and a resolution was passed removing the petitioner as a director of LSE. A and G transferred most of LSE's students to CTC and made an agreement with an American university to grant recognition of a BSc degree course to CTC and not LSE. The petitioner set up a rival institution (LCEE) in the same centre as CTC and took 12 LSE students with him. The petitioner sought a purchase order for his shares in LSE, alleging that the conduct of the respondents had been unfairly prejudicial to his interests.

Held The order would be granted. The conduct of CTC in appropriating to itself students from LSE was clearly both unfair and prejudicial to the interests of the petitioner as a member of the company. The court was empowered by s 75 of the CA 1980 to grant such relief as it thought fit if it was satisfied that the company's affairs were being, or had been, conducted in a manner unfairly prejudicial to the interests of some part of the members. The conduct of the petitioner could affect the relief so granted. However, there was no requirement that it should be just or equitable to grant relief or that the petitioner should come to the court with clean hands.

As to the question of valuation the date at which the valuation would be made would be the date of the presentation of the petition and on the basis that the students removed by the petitioner had in fact remained with the company. The petitioners shares should be valued on a *pro rata* basis and should not be discounted as a minority shareholding.

Re Cumana Ltd (1986) CA

The company was jointly owned by L (who held one-third of the shares) and B (who held the remaining two-thirds of the shares). L brought a petition for relief under s 75 of the CA 1980 alleging unfair prejudice and asking for a purchase order for his shares in the company. The trial judge accepted L's version of the facts (which were in dispute). L and B had entered into an agreement involving mutual trust and confidence which had been broken by B's actions. B had diverted business from the company to another company, procured the company to make a rights issue so as to reduce L's proportionate holding, and paid himself an excessive salary. This had caused unfair prejudice to L. B appealed.

Held The appeal was dismissed by the Court of Appeal. The judge had been correct to accept the facts as alleged by L. The actions of B had caused unfair prejudice to L and thus he was entitled to the relief sought. B had awarded himself remuneration of £265,000 over a 14-month period. This was clearly excessive and was correctly held to be unfairly prejudicial to the petitioner's interests. The rights issue, which would have reduced the petitioner's shareholding from one-third to less than 5%, was also unfairly prejudicial in itself.

Re Sam Weller Ltd (1990)

The petitioners were the owners of around 43% of the issued share capital of a family company. The company was run by Sam Weller. In recent years, the company had become increasingly profitable. However, the dividend declared each year remained as it had done for the last 37 years. The petitioners alleged, *inter alia*, that the failure to approve the payment of larger dividends amounted to unfairly prejudicial conduct. Sam Weller applied to have the petition struck out by reason of the fact that the conduct alleged affected all members equally and could not therefore be unfairly prejudicial to the interests of some part of the members.

Held The application was dismissed because members might have different interests even if their rights as members were effectively the same. Conduct could be unfairly prejudicial within the meaning of s 459 notwithstanding that it affected all the members equally. Where conduct prejudiced all members equally, it could still be held to be unfairly prejudicial to the interests of some part of the members. The payment of low dividends was capable of amounting to conduct unfairly prejudicial to some of the members, including the petitioners.

Re Elgindata Ltd (1991)

The shares of the company were held by the R and his wife, and P. R was a director of the company until relations between himself and P broke down and R resigned from the board. R brought a petition under s 459 of the CA 1985 for a share purchase order, alleging that P's conduct in controlling the affairs of the company had been unfairly prejudicial to R and his wife's interests. The allegations were, *inter alia*, that P had managed the company incompetently and that he had misused company assets for his own personal and family benefit.

Held The purchase order was granted. P had improperly used the company's assets for his own personal and family benefit. Although the impact of this on the value of the petitioner's interests was limited, it was enough to constitute unfairly prejudicial conduct. The allegations of mismanagement were not, however, sufficient for the court to find them unfairly prejudicial. The court would be reluctant to hold mismanagement to be unfairly prejudicial unless it was proved in an appropriate case to have been serious.

8.3.3 Section 459 and public companies

Re Blue Arrow plc (1987)

The company was originally owned to the extent of a 45% shareholding by the petitioner, who was an executive director of the company and was also appointed president. The company was floated on the Unlisted Securities Market and adopted articles of association suitable for a public company. The company grew and became a public company, with the consequence that the petitioner's shareholding was reduced to a mere 2.1% The other directors proposed to alter the company's articles so that the board could remove the petitioner from her post as president by majority vote. The petitioner presented a petition under s 459 of the CA 1985 alleging unfairly prejudicial conduct in that she had a legitimate expectation that she would continue to participate in the affairs of the company. The respondent moved to have the petition struck out.

Held The petition was struck out. The interests of a member of a company were not limited to the strict legal rights conferred by the company's constitution. The court could pay regard to wider equitable considerations in deciding the interests of a member. On the facts, however, the outside investors were entitled to assume that the whole of the company's constitution would be contained in the company's articles and relevant legislation. There was no basis, therefore, for finding that the petitioner had a legitimate expectation that the articles of the company would not be altered in order for her office to be terminated in a way other than that provided for by the articles.

8.3.4   Valuation

Re Bird Precision Bellows Ltd (1984) CA
The petitioners had been directors of the company until their removal from office. They alleged that the company was in effect a quasi-partnership and that there had been an understanding that they would participate in the conduct of the company's affairs. Their removal therefore constituted their wrongful exclusion from the conduct of the company's business. The petition under s 75 of the CA 1980 alleged that the affairs of the company had been conducted in a manner unfairly prejudicial to them, and requested that the respondents purchase the petitioners' shares.

Held The order was granted and the matter which arose was how to value the petitioners' shares. The court decided that if the sale was being forced because of the unfairly prejudicial conduct of the majority, and the shares had been acquired on the incorporation of a quasi-partnership company in which the petitioners had a legitimate expectation that they would participate, the price should be fixed on a *pro rata* basis. If the petitioners had conducted themselves so as to deserve exclusion from the company's affairs, the price should be discounted as if they had elected to sell their shares. In the instant case, the petitioners had been wrongfully excluded and thus the price should be fixed on a *pro rata* basis. The date for valuation was the date of the order.

8.3.5   Relationship between s 459 relief and derivative claim

Lowe v Fahey (1995)
The petitioner, Mrs Lowe, owned one share in Fahey Developments Ltd, a property development company which was the third respondent in this case. The other issued share in Fahey Developments Ltd was owned by her sister-in-law, Mrs Fahey, who was the second respondent in this case, the first respondent being Mr Fahey. It was Mr Lowe and Mr Fahey who were directors of the company and ran Fahey Developments Ltd for all intents and purposes. Brickfield Property Ltd, the fourth respondent in these proceedings, was an Irish company which was assumed, for the purposes of these proceedings, to be owned and controlled by the Faheys. Mrs Lowe brought a s 459 petition alleging that the Faheys had used Brickfield Ltd as a vehicle for siphoning off profits which should rightly have gone

to Fahey Developments Ltd – it alleged mismanagement and breach of fiduciary duty on the part of Mr Fahey. The petition sought an order that Mr and Mrs Fahey and Brickfield Property Ltd account to Fahey Developments Ltd for any sums that may be found to be due to it and also that, in the case of Mr Fahey, he be ordered to pay damages to Fahey Developments Ltd for breach of fiduciary duty, and also that the court declare a property bought by Brickfield Property Ltd, with moneys allegedly diverted from Fahey Developments Ltd, to be held on trust for it. Brickfield Property Ltd applied to court for the s 459 petition against it to be struck out arguing that the relief sought in the petition against it could not properly be awarded under s 461 but rather was simply a derivative action in the name of the company disguised as a s 459 petition.

Held The court refused to strike out the petition holding that it was quite in order for a s 459 petitioner, where the unfairly prejudicial conduct complained of involved diversion of company property, to seek an order under s 461 for payment to the company itself, and such relief could be sought not only against those involved in the unlawful diversion but also against third parties who have knowingly received such property or dishonestly assisted in its diversion.

9 Shares, share capital and debentures

9.1 Shares

9.1.1 Nature of shares

Borland's Trustee v Steel Bros & Co Ltd (1901)
Mr Borland had 73 £100 shares in the defendant company. The company's articles of association provided that on the occurrence of certain specified events, including the bankruptcy of a member, that member's shares should be compulsorily transferable to specified persons upon payment of a fair price which was not to exceed par value. Mr Borland was declared bankrupt and his Trustee in Bankruptcy brought an action seeking a declaration that the compulsory transfer provision in the articles was void on the grounds that it was inconsistent with the concept of absolute ownership or void for offending perpetuity.

Held The trustee's argument failed. Mr Justice Farwell said that it rested on a misconception of what a share really is and that 'A share is the interest of a shareholder in the company measured by a sum of money, for the purpose of liability in the first place, and of interest in the second, but also consisting of a series of mutual covenants entered into by all the shareholders *inter se* in accordance … with the Companies Act'. He said that owning a share did not equate to owning a sum of money absolutely subject to certain limitations (as was argued by the plaintiff) but rather was better seen as owning an interest which was measured by a sum of money but was made up of various rights contained in the articles of association.

Bradbury v English Sewing Cotton Co Ltd (1923) HL
The House of Lords examined the nature of shares and said that a share is a fractional part of the share capital. Shares are also the individual property of all the members but this does not mean that all the members as a group own the share capital. The share capital is something different from all the shares aggregated. The share capital belongs to the company.

9.1.2 Share certificates

Re Bahia and San Francisco Rly Co (1868) CQB

T owned five shares in the company. X and Y forged a transfer of the shares to themselves and lodged the transfer and T's share certificate with the company, which duly entered X and Y as the registered members and issued a fresh share certificate bearing their names. All this took place without T's knowledge. B and G purchased the shares in good faith on the stock exchange. They were registered as the new owners and issued with fresh share certificates. However, T brought a successful action to rectify the register of members and B and G then duly brought an action for equivalent shares or damages against the company.

Held B and G were awarded damages. The court held that the company was estopped from denying the statement it had made in the share certificate relied upon that X and Y were the owners of the shares. A share certificate is *prima facie* evidence of title.

Burkinshaw v Nicholls (1878) HL

A company is estopped from denying statements made in its share certificates. So if it mistakenly says on the face of the share certificate that shares were issued fully paid up then the company cannot demand further payment on those shares (and indeed must treat the shares as fully paid for all purposes) from anyone who has purchased or provided security on those shares relying on the truth of what is stated in the certificate.

9.1.3 Restrictions on transfer of shares

Re Smith & Fawcett Ltd (1942) CA

The company's articles of association provided that the directors might in their absolute and uncontrolled discretion refuse to register any transfer of the company's shares. The company had only two directors, Mr Smith and Mr Fawcett, who held 4,001 shares each. After Fawcett's death Smith and a co-opted director refused to register a transfer of his shares into the names of his executors or one of the executors. Instead, Mr Smith offered to register the transfer of 2,001 shares and to buy the remaining 2,000 shares himself.

Held The Court of Appeal refused to intervene in the directors' exercise of discretion to refuse to register the transfer. The court examined the general position on transferability of private company shares. They emphasised that the starting point for the law was always that a free right of alienability attached to shares and if that was to be cut down in any way then it must be done so with sufficient clarity. The language of this particular article was simple – the directors had the power to refuse registration – the language used did not qualify that power in any way. The court thought it significant that this type of article was commonly found in other private companies with various qualifications attached to the power to refuse, but in this case there were no such qualifications or restrictions so the power was indeed absolute.

Berry and Stewart v Tottenham Hotspur Football and Athletic Co Ltd (1935)

Mr Berry had one share in the defendant company which he transferred to Mr Stewart, but on subsequently attempting to register the transfer they were met with a refusal to register it by the directors. Under the defendant company's articles of association, the directors had power to refuse registration of a transfer on four specific grounds, and were not obliged to declare on which ground the refusal was based. The plaintiffs attempted to find out which ground the refusal was based on.

Held Where the directors power to refuse registration is unlimited and absolute, ie there are no grounds specified in the articles upon which a refusal must be based, then the directors are not under any duty to state the reasons for their decision. Even when, as here, the articles did specify specific grounds for refusal the transferee need not be told which ground a refusal is based on if the articles, as here, so provide.

Re Coalport China Co (1895) CA

The company was a family company and one of its articles of association gave the directors power to refuse to register a transfer if, in their opinion, the transferee was not a desirable person to admit to membership of the company. They refused to register a transfer to an outsider of the share of one of the original subscribers to the company's memorandum. They offered no reason for the refusal and the transferee and transferor brought an action for rectification of the register.

Held The Court of Appeal said that where it was argued that the directors have exercised their power improperly then the onus of proof lay on those seeking to challenge the exercise of the power.

Re Bede Steam Shipping Company Ltd (1917)

The company's articles of association contained a power for the directors to refuse to register a transfer of shares if '... in their opinion it is contrary to the interests of the company that the proposed transferee should be a member thereof ...'. Three brothers were shareholders in the company; one of the brothers was in dispute with the other two and he sold two fully paid ordinary shares to two other individuals. The other two brothers (who were also directors) refused to register the transfers on the general grounds that they did not think it was in the interests of the company that small lots of shares be allocated to outsiders with no interest in or knowledge of the company's affairs. They made it clear that the refusal in no way reflected on the character or financial standing of the two proposed transferees. The directors decision was duly challenged.

Held The court started by re-iterating the principle of free transferability of a company's shares subject to any restrictions contained in the company's articles. The court said that any challenge to the exercise of directors powers to refuse registration must be approached via a three-stage analysis:

- What is the power vested in the directors?
- Did they exercise or purport to exercise that power?
- Was their action *bona fide* and in the interests of the company or arbitrary and capricious?

The court examined the power in question in this case and said that the nature of a power such as this one was that it must be exercised with respect to the transferee the motives of the transferor are irrelevant. For the power to be properly exercised, it must be exercised with reference to factor(s) personal to the transferee. That had not happened in this particular case – the directors had simply assumed from the names and addresses of the transferees and the peppercorn consideration paid for the shares themselves that they would hold the shares as nominees for the third brother. The directors made no attempt to ascertain any further information about the purported transferees. Hence, the court held it was an improper exercise of the actual power vested in the directors and the court ordered registration of the transfers – there was no need to go into the third stage of the analysis and examine the question of whether their action was *bona fide* and in the interests of the company.

Re Swaledale Cleaners Ltd (1968) CA

The company's articles of association contained a provision whereby the directors had power to refuse to register a transfer of shares. In August 1967, S owned 4,000 of the company's shares, the applicant in this case owned 500 shares and two recently deceased members had owned between them 5,500 shares. Transfers of these 5,500 shares had been executed in favour of the applicant. The quorum necessary for the directors to validly transact business was two. S and the applicant were directors but at the AGM in August 1967 the applicant had to retire by rotation and was not re-appointed as director; when the transfers were produced for registration this was refused. Since S was the sole director at this point, the directors meeting was not quorate and hence the refusal was invalid. Four months later the applicant brought an action for rectification of the register of members. A few days after this, S took action to appoint an additional director so the directors' meeting was now quorate and it refused to register the transfer of shares to the applicant.

Held It was too late – the power to refuse registration had lapsed as it had not been validly exercised within a reasonable time after the transfer had been submitted. Rectification was ordered. Lord Justice Harman said that, all other things being equal, a reasonable time for these purposes would be taken to be two months – the equivalent time period specified in s 183(5) of the Companies Act (CA) 1985 within which directors must notify of a decision to refuse registration.

Popely v Planarrive Ltd (1996)

The company's articles of association gave the directors absolute discretion to refuse to register transfers of shares without need to give reasons. They also obliged directors to notify the transferee of refusal of his transfer within two months of the transfer being lodged. A directors' meeting at which a transfer of shares to the applicant had been refused had been held within two months of the transfer being lodged with the company but the result of the meeting had not been notified to the applicant within the time period stated.

Held This breach did not invalidate the directors' decision to refuse to register the transfer. That earlier decision had been validly made and although failure to give timely notification of it to the applicant might expose the directors to civil or criminal penalties it would not undo a decision which had been properly taken on the basis of an unqualified and absolute power, the only qualification on it being that the directors act *bona fide* in the interests of the company.

Re Hackney Pavilion Ltd (1924)

The company had three directors who each owned one-third of the issued share capital. One director died and his widow applied for registration of a transfer of her late husband's shares from herself as executrix to herself beneficially. The two remaining directors met – one proposed the transfer and the other objected – there being no provision for a casting vote the widow was informed that the company had declined to register the transfer.

Held Rectification of the register of members was ordered in the widow's favour as the right to decline registration had not been positively exercised – the fact that the resolution to register the transfer was not passed was not the same thing as an active exercise of the directors' right to refuse registration.

Stothers v William Steward (Holdings) Ltd (1994) CA

The question before the court was the interpretation of regs 30–31 of Table A of the Companies Act 1948 and the relationship between directors' rights to refuse registration of transfers of shares and transmission of shares of a deceased shareholder as provided for in his will. Did the articles give the personal representatives of a deceased shareholder the right to transmission of his shares to the beneficiary named in his will or did the directors of the company have the right to refuse registration of the transfer of shares to the beneficiary?

Held Company law drew a distinction between the transfer of shares and the transmission of shares on death of a shareholder and accordingly the directors' right to refuse registration of transfer did not apply.

Lyle & Scott Ltd v Scott's Trustees (1959) HL

The appellant company's articles of association provided that any member 'desirous of transferring his shares' should serve a transfer notice upon the company, service of which would set in motion certain pre-emption procedures whereby the other members of the company would have the right to buy those shares at a price fixed by the company's auditor. Some of the registered shareholders entered into binding specifically enforceable contracts of sale with third parties under which they received £3 for each £1 share held and which also bound them to vote these shares as the third parties directed. Short of becoming the registered owner of the shares themselves the third parties were thus as in control of the shares as it was possible for them to be.

Held The House of Lords ruled that this scheme was ineffective as a means of avoiding the operation of the pre-emption provision contained in the company's articles. For a shareholder who agrees to sell his shares and retains the price he receives in return for such an agreement must be 'desirous of transferring his shares' within the meaning of the pre-emption article. The word 'transfer' here did not refer just to the complete transfer of legal ownership of the shares but rather was used in its ordinary and natural meaning of 'parting with something' or 'handing something over'. The shareholders party to these agreements were thus ordered to serve a transfer notice on the company as required by the pre-emption article.

Safeguard Industrial Investments Ltd v National Westminster Bank (1982) CA
The appellant company's articles of association required that a 'proposing transferor' of its shares had to give notice to the company which set-off a pre-emption procedure in favour of existing members. The respondent bank were executors of a deceased shareholder's will which had left his shareholding to two persons who thereby would gain effective control of the appellant company. The bank would on completion of the administration of the estate hold the deceased's shares on trust for the two beneficiaries. The beneficiaries asked the bank not to transfer legal title in the shares to them but to retain it and to hold the shares as their nominee. Other members of the company argued that the combined effect of the will and the bank's trusteeship for the beneficiaries was, in the light of the House of Lords' decision in *Lyle & Scott Ltd*, to constitute the bank a 'proposing transferor' within the meaning of the pre-emption article.

Held This was a wholly different situation to that which prevailed in *Lyle & Scott Ltd*. Here the bank was under an involuntarily assumed obligation to transfer legal title in the shares should the beneficiaries under the will ever require it, whereas in *Lyle & Scott* the members had been under a voluntarily undertaken consensual obligation to transfer title to the third parties. In this context, the word 'transfer' as used in the pre-emption article meant transfer of legal title to the shares not transfer of beneficial interest.

9.1.4 Disclosure of interests in shares

Re Geers Gross plc (1988)

Geers Gross plc had agreed with an individual, Mr E, that he would not acquire more than 20% of its issued share capital. Subsequent to this agreement, Geers Gross plc suspected that Mr E might have breached this agreement through indirect acquisitions of its shares by those who it suspected to be acting as his nominees. About 3% of its share capital had been bought by a nominee company ostensibly on behalf of a Swiss bank. Geers Gross plc therefore served notices pursuant to s 212 of the CA 1985 on both the nominee and the Swiss bank. Both refused to comply with the notices and so Geers Gross plc obtained an order restricting transfer of that 3% shareholding. The nominee company and the Swiss bank applied to court for the order to be lifted as they now wished to sell and part with all interest in these shares.

Held The order sought was refused as the court held that Geers Gross plc's s 212 right to investigate who was interested in its shares was an unqualified right and would be impossible to pursue if the order restricting transfer of the shares was lifted. Hence, the order restricting transfer of the shareholding was to remain in force until the bank and nominee company complied with the s 212 request made to them.

Meridian Global Funds Management Asia Ltd v Securities Commission (1995) PC

See Chapter 2, above, 2.11.

9.2 Capital

9.2.1 A company can have a share capital denominated in any currency

Re Scandinavian Bank plc

The company wished to restructure its share capital so as to consist of shares denominated in four different currencies: £30 million (sterling), 30 million DM, 30 million Swiss Francs and 30 million US Dollars. The motive behind this restructuring was to better reflect the underlying composition of the company's assets. Section 2(5) of the CA 1985 states that every company must show the 'amount of the share capital divided into shares of a fixed amount' in its memorandum of association. The questions before the court were:

- whether these words in s 2(5) meant that the memorandum had to state a single figure for the total of the share capital; and
- whether the share capital had to be denominated in sterling or whether it could be denominated in fixed amounts of foreign currencies.

Held Mr Justice Harman held that the words used in s 2(5) do not require that the share capital be stated in one single total amount but rather it could be divided into several fixed amounts – so long as they were each expressed in recognised monetary units. Also, it was quite in order for a company to have share capital expressed in different fixed amounts of non-sterling currencies. The only restriction as to currency contained in the Companies legislation was the requirement in ss 117–18 of the CA 1985 that public companies have a minimum issued nominal capital of £50,000 and that requirement was satisfied here.

9.3   Debentures and loan capital

9.3.1   Nature of debentures

Levy v Abercorris Slate and Slab Co (1887)
The plaintiff's claim against the defendant was based upon an instrument that the defendant argued was void under the Bills of Sale Act (1878) Amendment Act 1882 whereas the plaintiff argued that it was a 'debenture' and therefore exempt from the strictures of that legislation. The court was therefore required to pronounce on the definition of 'debenture'.

Held Chitty J said that a debenture was a document which either created a debt or acknowledged it so that any document which fulfilled either of those conditions was a 'debenture'.

British India Steam Navigation Co v IRC (1881)
The company had issued instruments whereby the company promised to pay the holder of such an instrument £100 on 30 November 1882 and 5% interest half-yearly. The instruments were not under seal and in order to avoid a higher rate of stamp duty the company argued that they were not debentures but rather promissory notes.

Held The court disagreed. However, the court declined to ascribe a precise definition to the term debenture but made it clear it was capable of encompassing many different forms of instrument and an instrument not being under seal was no bar to its being a debenture.

10 Raising and maintaining capital

10.1 Allotment of shares

10.1.1 Meaning of 'allotment'

National Westminster Bank plc v IRC; Barclays Bank plc v IRC (1995) HL
These two tax appeals concerned the interpretation of the term 'issue' when used in the context of shares being issued for the purposes of computing tax relief under the Business Expansion Scheme. The question for the court was – is an allotment of shares something different in law from an issue of shares? If so, then at what stage in the post-allotment process could shares be said to be issued?

Held The two terms were distinguishable – allotment was the stage at which the company and allottee became contractually bound to issue the shares whereas the shares could only be said to be issued at a later stage – when the allottee's legal title had been perfected by the company effecting registration of the allottee or his nominee as the owner of the shares.

Nicol's Case (1885) CA
W had applied for shares in the company and had been sent a letter of allotment by the company calling on him to pay a sum due on allotment. The money was never paid and W's name was never put on the company's register of members. Three years later the directors of the company cancelled the allotment and then all of the company's shares comprised in its nominal capital were issued to others. When the company subsequently went into liquidation, the liquidator sought to make W liable as a contributory.

Held The Court of Appeal agreed with the first instance ruling that W was not liable. He had never acquired the status of member of the company since his name had not been entered in the register of members of the company. There had been for a time a valid and enforceable contract of allotment between W and the company, but that contract had, by lapse of time and the conduct of the company in cancelling and re-allotting the shares, been rescinded.

Ramsgate Victoria Hotel Co Ltd v Montefiore (1866) (Court of Exchequer)
The defendants applied for shares in the company on 8 June but no allotment was made by the company until 23 November, by which time the defendants were refusing to accept the shares.

Held The defendants were entitled to take this position since their application for the shares had lapsed as the allotment to them had not been made within a reasonable time.

10.1.2 Directors' power to allot shares must be exercised *bona fide* and in the interests of the company

Hogg v Cramphorn (1967)
See Chapter 5, above, 5.4.3.

Howard Smith v Ampol Petroleum Ltd (1974) PC
See Chapter 5, above, 5.4.3.

10.1.3 Pricing of and payment for shares

Ooregum Gold Mining Co of India v Roper (1892) HL
This case concerned an action brought by one of the appellant company's ordinary shareholders challenging the validity of an issue of preference shares made by the directors on the basis that each new share of £1 nominal value would be credited as three-quarters paid leaving a liability to pay up the remaining quarter. The question for the court was – could the company arrange with the shareholders that they would not be liable for the unpaid amount?

Held The House of Lords forbade this scheme. They said that the nominal value of a share is a fixed and certain amount to which every creditor of the company is entitled to look for his security, therefore, shares must never be issued at a discount to their nominal value.

Moseley v Koffyfontein Mines Ltd (1904) CA
The company's share capital was divided into 125,000 shares with a nominal value of one shilling each. The directors were proposing to allot 5% debentures in denominations of 10, 25, 50 and 100 shillings. However, the proposal was to allot the debentures at 80% of their nominal value, so a 100 shilling debenture would cost only 80 shillings, and the debenture-holder would then be able to direct the company at any time to allot to him in exchange for his debenture fully paid shares in the company at an exchange rate of a one shilling share for every one shilling of the nominal amount of the debenture.

Held The Court of Appeal rejected this scheme saying that even if it was not a sham indirect discounted share issue, even if it was honestly made by the company in good faith and in expectation that the debentureholders would retain their debentures rather than convert them into shares it still contravened the principle that a company must receive in money or money's worth the full nominal value of a share in return for the allotment of that share.

Hilder v Dexter (1902) HL

After the company in question was incorporated, it issued one-sixth of the shares comprised in its nominal capital which had a par value of £1 each. These shares were issued at par value on the basis that the shareholders would have an option to take up further shares in the company at par value on a one for one basis. When the shares were worth £2.87, the appellant sought to exercise this now quite valuable option to subscribe for further shares for only £1. The respondent, who was another shareholder in the company, obtained an injunction restraining the exercise of the option on the grounds that this arrangement contravened what is now s 98 of the CA 1985.

Held The House of Lords allowed the appeal and lifted the injunction. The advantage which the appellant obtained from the exercise of his option was not obtained at the expense of the company's capital, it was not a prohibited discount or allowance. Simply because a company could obtain a price above par value for its shares does not mean that it is obliged by law to do so – that is a question for the directors to decide.

Re Wragg Ltd (1897) CA

W and M sold their unincorporated business to the newly incorporated Wragg Ltd for £46,300. The purchase price was part in cash and debentures and part in the form of the allotment to W and M of the company's nominal capital as fully paid shares. When the company subsequently went into liquidation, the liquidator argued that the original purchase price of £46,300 was too high in that it had overvalued the business by £18,000 and he claimed that W and M be liable to pay up that amount on shares held by them or be liable to contribute to the company's debts in that amount on the grounds of directors' misfeasance.

Held The liquidator's claim failed. Other than the prohibition of issuing shares at a discount to par value, it is no business of company law to inquire into the adequacy of consideration that a company agrees to pay in return for an allotment of its shares. Lindley LJ said, 'It has ... never yet been decided that a limited company cannot buy property or pay for services at any price it thinks proper, and pay for them in fully paid-up shares.'

10.2 Wrongful payment of dividends

Re Exchange Banking Co, Flitcroft's Case (1882) CA

The directors of the company had prepared and presented accounts to the shareholders which showed what were in fact (and the directors knew to

be) bad debts owed to the company as assets of the company. On the
strength of these accounts, the shareholders had, for several years,
approved the payment of dividends by the company when in fact the company had no profits available for distribution as dividend. The dividends
had thus been wrongfully paid and the liquidator of the company sought
to have the directors made personally liable for to the company for the
amounts of dividend wrongfully so paid.

Held The liquidator's claim succeeded. Jessel MR firmly stated the doctrine of capital maintenance and the creditor protection rationale behind it.
He said that since the directors were quasi-trustees for the company then
they were liable to repay to the company any assets improperly paid away.

Moxham v Grant (1900)

A company's directors made an unlawful distribution of capital to the
company's shareholders. The shareholders knew that this was an unlawful payment out of capital and the company's liquidators recovered the
amounts so paid from the directors who now in turn sought an indemnity
from the shareholders who had received the payments.

Held The court granted the directors the indemnity sought. The court
said that the shareholders received the payment as constructive trustees in
these circumstances and drew an analogy with trusteeship in that the
directors could be seen as their co-trustees being entitled to indemnity for
a breach of trust.

Precision Dippings Ltd v Precision Dippings Marketing Ltd (1985) CA

The plaintiff company was a wholly owned subsidiary of the defendant
company and paid the defendant a cash dividend of £60,000. The accounts
which related to the period in which this payment of dividend was made
showed sufficient distributable profits to pay this dividend but these
accounts had also been qualified by the auditors. However, that qualification had not been stated to be material by the auditors as required by the
Companies Act. The plaintiff company subsequently went into liquidation
and the liquidator tried to recover the dividend payment made, arguing
that it was paid in contravention of the Companies Act and was therefore
ultra vires.

Held The claim succeeded. The Court of Appeal held that the fact that
the auditors had not supplied the written statement as to materiality of
their qualification of the accounts before the dividend payment was made
was more than a mere procedural irregularity – it rendered the payment of
the dividend *ultra vires* and since the defendant company received the cash
as constructive trustee for the plaintiff, having notice of all the facts, it was
liable to repay the amount of dividend wrongfully paid.

companies providing him with a salary, pension and profit share from the net profits of the group of companies. The agreement did not specify the proportions of these payments to be made by each of the four companies. Three years later, the plaintiff sued Bridport and his sons, claiming arrears of payments due to him under the 1988 agreement. The defendants resisted the claim arguing that the 1988 agreement was illegal and unenforceable as it required Guppys (Estates) Ltd giving illegal financial assistance in order for the sons to acquire its shares. Its assets were reduced to a material extent by its becoming privy to the 1988 agreement to make the payments to the father and therefore s 151(1) of the CA 1985 had been contravened. This defence succeeded at first instance whereupon the plaintiff appealed to the Court of Appeal.

Held The plaintiff's appeal was successful. The Court of Appeal pointed out that the draftsman of ss 151–58 of the CA 1985 most probably did not have continuing financial assistance in mind but that did not mean such assistance could not fall within the statutory prohibition, it was simply more difficult to apply the provisions to such assistance. In this case, there was no need at all, on the facts, for Guppys (Estates) Ltd to make any contribution to the payments specified in the 1988 agreement – Guppys (Bridport) Ltd and Guppys (Properties) Ltd could easily have met the obligations themselves. Simply because the 1988 agreement was capable of performance in such a way as to constitute an infringement of s 151 did not mean that it actually was an infringement thereof. The Court of Appeal said, *obiter*, that what was 'material' for the purposes of a material reduction in net assets in s 152(1) should not be subject to any rule of thumb and was a question of degree to be answered by reference to the facts of a particular case.

10.4.2 Applicability of the s 153 exception

Brady v Brady (1988) HL

The Brady brothers ran a group of companies which had two limbs to its business – road haulage and drinks. The two brothers disagreed with each other so seriously that the business was becoming deadlocked, so the group was re-organised so that the business would be divided between them – one brother taking the drinks side the other the haulage. A complex scheme of reconstruction was drawn up under which assets were transferred from the principal company ('Brady Ltd') to a new company controlled by one brother in order to equalise the value of the two constituent parts of the business. This transfer involved the giving of financial assistance by Brady Ltd towards discharging the liability of its holding company, M Ltd, for the price of shares which M Ltd had bought in Brady Ltd. So in effect Brady Ltd was paying M Ltd to buy shares in Brady Ltd – the overall net effect was a shift in value from Brady Ltd to M

Ltd. *Prima facie,* this was a clear infringement of s 151. The agreement to reconstruct the group was never performed and the non-performing brother argued that the whole scheme constituted illegal financial assistance. The plaintiff brother, however, who was keen to see the agreement performed argued that the financial assistance was permissible in that it fell within the s 153 proviso as it was but an incidental purpose of a larger commercial purpose of the company, ie the breaking of the deadlock between the two brothers which was choking the whole business to death, hence the good faith/principal purpose in s 153 applied.

Held The House of Lords held that the s 153 proviso was not applicable here. They reasoned that what was asserted to be the broader commercial purpose of the company in entering into this scheme was in actual fact nothing more than the reason why it was entering into it. Lord Oliver said it was vital to draw a distinction between a purpose and a reason why a purpose is formed. The purpose of this transaction was to assist in financing the acquisition of the shares in Brady Ltd. Moreover, what was asserted to be a 'larger purpose' (within the meaning of s 153(2)) was not – it was merely a reason. Their Lordships did, however, order specific performance of the agreement on another ground – since Brady Ltd was a solvent private company, it could lawfully have given financial assistance by following the procedure available to private companies prescribed by ss 155–58.

10.4.3 Consequences of contravention of s 151

Victor Battery Co Ltd v Curry's Ltd (1946)

Mr J was a director of and the principal shareholder in two companies – B company and X company. Mr J agreed to buy the issued share capital of the plaintiff company for £15,000. Mr J was only able to find £6,000 of the purchase price but the defendant company helped him complete the purchase by lending £6,000 to B company, £2,000 to X company and £2,000 directly to the plaintiff company. The purchase went ahead and after completion the plaintiff company issued a debenture, for £10,000 to a nominee of the defendant company, thereby providing security for the defendant company's loans which assisted Mr J to buy the plaintiff's shares. When a receiver was appointed under the debenture the plaintiff company tried to get the debenture declared void and unenforceable as granting it constituted illegal financial assistance.

Held The statutory prohibition on financial assistance did not make the security granted illegal and unenforceable for the purpose of protecting borrowing companies in the position of the plaintiff company here. The statutory prohibition was there to punish them not to benefit them and they would be benefited if they could so rely on the illegality of the debenture so as to prevent its enforcement against them.

Heald v O'Connor (1971)

The defendant, Mr O'Connor, guaranteed a secured loan made by the plaintiffs to a company. The defendant also bought the plaintiffs' shares in that same company. The company subsequently defaulted on the loan and the plaintiffs sought to enforce the guarantee, given by the defendant. In an action for summary judgment on the guarantee the defendant asked for leave to defend on the ground that the loan had in fact been made to him to enable him to buy the shares in the company and the security thus granted by the company was, in these circumstances, void and illegal as being given in contravention of the financial assistance prohibition.

Held The court gave the defendant leave to defend, disagreeing with the decision in *Victor Battery Co Ltd v Curry's Ltd*. A debenture granted in contravention of the financial assistance provisions is illegal and void – the deterrent effect of so ruling is desirable as it will caution lenders from providing finance to schemes which might offend the statute.

Selangor United Rubber Estates Ltd v Cradock (No 3) (1968)

Mr Cradock had obtained a controlling interest in the plaintiff company. He had paid for this interest with the use of the plaintiff's own funds in contravention of statutory financial assistance provisions. Proceedings were now brought in the plaintiff company's name to recover the sums of its money improperly paid away in contravention of the statute by its directors who were fixed with knowledge of Cradock's improper purpose.

Held The directors were liable to the company for breach of trust, as constructive trustees despite the fact that the company itself was also party to the illegal transaction. The company's claim for breach of trust is against the directors for perpetrating the illegal transaction and making the company a party to it. The illegality of the transaction does not prevent the company being reimbursed money paid by it unlawfully pursuant to a transaction to which it was party.

10.5 Company cannot make unauthorised return of capital to shareholders

Aveling Barford Ltd v Perion Ltd (1989) CA

The plaintiff and defendant companies were both owned by the same individual. Aveling Barford Ltd was not insolvent at the material time but neither did it have profits available for distribution. It owned a plot of land which had recently been valued at £650,000. It was decided to sell the land to Perion Ltd for £350,000. Before it was sold, it was revalued at £1.15 million. Perion Ltd resold it within a year for £1.52 million. The liquidator of Aveling Barford Ltd brought an action for the proceeds of that sale.

Held The liquidator's application was granted. Mr Justice Hoffmann characterised the transaction as an unauthorised return of capital which was *ultra vires* and incapable of validation by shareholder consent and approval. He said:

> The general rule is that any act which falls within the express or implied powers of a company conferred by its memorandum of association, whether or not a breach of duty on the part of the directors, will be binding on the company if it is approved or subsequently ratified by the shareholders: see *Rolled Steel Products (Holdings) Ltd v British Steel Corporation*. But this rule is subject to exceptions created by the general law and one such exception is that a company cannot, without the leave of the court or the adoption of a special procedure, return its capital to its shareholders. It follows that a transaction which amounts to an unauthorised return of capital is *ultra vires* and cannot be validated by shareholder ratification or approval. Whether or not the transaction is a distribution to shareholders does not depend exclusively on what the parties choose to call it.

11   Changing capital structure

11.1   Class rights and variation

11.1.1   What is a class right?

Cumbrian Newspapers Group Ltd v Cumberland and Westmoreland Herald Newspaper and Printing Group Ltd (1986)

The plaintiff company had, as part of a scheme of amalgamation, acquired 10.67% of the ordinary shares of the defendant company. In order to make it difficult for anyone outside the Cumbrian Newspapers Group Ltd to ever gain control of newspapers owned by the defendant company, the articles of association of the defendant company were altered so that the plaintiff company had three types of special right attaching to any ordinary shares it held in the defendant at any time. These three categories of rights were: (1) rights of pre-emption on the transfer of any other issued ordinary shares in the defendant company; (2) pre-emption rights over any unissued shares in the defendant company; (3) the right to appoint a director of the defendant so long as the plaintiff owned at least 10% of its shares. The question before the court was – if the company wanted to alter those particular articles, did this constitute a variation of class rights even though the 'class' was defined by reference to any ordinary shares held by one person?

Held These rights, although they did not attach to particular shares but inured to an individual, were still capable of being 'class rights'.

11.1.2   Meaning of variation

White v Bristol Aeroplane Ltd (1953) CA

The company had preference shares and ordinary shares. A bonus issue was proposed of both preference and ordinary shares which would have the effect of proportionately increasing the number of ordinary shares in issue in relation to the preference shares in issue. The literal voting rights of both classes were unaffected by the bonus issue but the ordinary shareholders relative voting strength was increased afterwards simply because there were more of them. The preference shareholders challenged the bonus issue arguing that it constituted a variation of their class rights and they should have the protection of the s 125 procedure.

Held The Court of Appeal rejected the preference shareholders' argument. Their voting power as a class may be affected but their literal rights remained the same after the bonus issue as before. It was the enjoyment of the right that had been affected, not the legal nature of the right itself.

11.1.3 Class meeting to vote in the interests of the class

Carruth v ICI Ltd (1936) HL

The company had a large class of ordinary shares and a small class of deferred shares. A variation of the rights of the deferred shares was proposed as part of a reduction of capital scheme whereby the deferred shares would be consolidated with the ordinary shares and lose their preferential rights to surplus assets in a winding up. A separate class meeting of the deferred shareholders was called as required by s 125. However 80% of the deferred shareholders were also substantial members of the ordinary class of shareholders with holdings of ordinary shareholders far outweighing their deferred holdings. They approved the variation of the rights of the deferred shares since it was in their interests as ordinary shareholders so to do. The minority members of the deferred class challenged the fairness of the whole scheme, arguing that the procedural protections of the s 125 variation of rights provisions break down when the members of one class vote in the interests not of that class but of another class.

Held Despite the general rule that shareholders were better judges of their own advantage than the courts, in these particular circumstances, where it was proved that the majority of a class may have voted in the way that they did because of their interests as shareholders of another class then, in deciding the overall question of 'fairness' as between different classes of shareholders in a reduction of capital, little regard should be paid to the ostensibly independent s 125 class vote. However, the discretion of the court to override and disregard a class vote is not a technical one (ie it does not arise simply because the numbers are such that a majority of the class are also members of another class), rather its exercise has to be grounded on evidence that the proposed reduction is actually unfair to the class and the class vote approving it was brought about by the majority considering their own collateral interests rather than the interests of the class as a whole.

Re Holders Investment Trust Ltd (1971)

The company proposed to reduce its capital by cancelling its 5% cumulative preference shares in exchange for an equivalent amount of unsecured loan stock. Almost 90% of the preference shares were vested in trustees and trusts set up by one individual. They also held 52% of the ordinary stock and shares; they voted in favour of the proposal clearly influenced by the benefit they would receive as ordinary shareholders from the proposed scheme.

Held The scheme was unfair; Megarry J refused to sanction the reduction.

11.2 Reducing capital

11.2.1 Role of court

Ex parte Westburn Sugar Refineries Ltd (1951) HL

The government of the day was proposing to nationalise Westburn Sugar Refineries Ltd. The company had valuable investment holdings among its assets which it was keen to keep out of the forthcoming nationalisation of its sugar business, so it transferred these investment assets to an investment holding company especially formed for the purpose in return for being allotted shares in that company. Westburn Sugar Refineries Ltd then reduced the nominal value of all its ordinary shares from £1 to 18 shillings and all its ordinary shareholders received a two shilling nominal value share in the new investment holding company as part of that reduction. However, the investment assets actually held by the investment holding company (which represented indirectly the capital being returned to the Westburn shareholders) were worth a great deal more than just two shillings per share. The Scottish High Court would not allow this scheme on the grounds that the actual value of the capital assets being returned was far in excess of the nominal value of the capital sought to be reduced.

Held The House of Lords said that this was immaterial, what mattered was not the value of the investments which the company proposed to transfer but, rather, the value of the assets which it would retain. The court must ask, in its examination of a proposed reduction of capital, whether the rights of the creditors of the company are prejudiced and whether shareholders have been treated fairly, in particular if the proposed reduction deals with different classes of members fairly and equitably. Subject to making those enquiries, though, it was not the place of the court to enquire into the company's motive for a reduction.

Re Thorn EMI plc (1989)

The proposed reduction of capital involved the company taking money out of its share premium account in order that it could establish a special reserve account against which it could set-off goodwill arising in future years.

Held Mr Justice Harman listed the factors that a court must examine on any proposed reduction as being: (1) Are shareholders treated equitably? (2) Have the reduction proposals been properly explained to shareholders?

(3) Have the interests of creditors been safeguarded? (4) Is the reduction for a discernible purpose? It is important to distinguish between 'purpose' and 'motive', the company's motive for a reduction is not of concern to the court. The court is only concerned to see if there is a rationale or commercial reason for the reduction and in this case Harman J was happy to accept that saving time and costs in future years constituted a discernible purpose on the part of Thorn EMI plc for the reduction.

11.2.2 Treatment of different classes of shareholders in a reduction of capital

Scottish Insurance Co Ltd v Wilson & Clyde Coal Co Ltd (1949) HL
The company's colliery assets had been nationalised by the government and the company was left with its remaining non-colliery assets, since there was surplus value it was about to go into solvent liquidation. It had two classes of shares, preference shares and ordinary shares, the preference shares having a preferential right to dividend and also to repayment of capital contributed in a winding up. The company proposed a scheme for the reduction of capital by simply paying back the preference shareholders the capital they had contributed and cancelling them as a class. This was opposed by some preference shareholders on the grounds that it was unfair and inequitable since it would preclude them from sharing in any subsequent distribution of surplus assets. They argued that they had rights to share in a distribution of surplus assets and this reduction of capital scheme denied them any possibility of exercising those rights in the future and was thus unfair and inequitable.

Held The House of Lords held: (1) As a matter of law a statement of the rights attaching to the preference shares is an exhaustive statement of those rights, and so, if the articles of association state (as they did in this case) that the preference shares have priority as to repayment of capital contributed in a winding up then that is an exhaustive statement of their rights as to capital. They are to have no further rights to participate in a surplus of assets in a winding up. (2) In any event, whether or not these particular preference shares had any surplus rights was irrelevant to the question of was the reduction of capital unfair and inequitable? The House of Lords said that the company had followed the proper procedures on a reduction and the preference shareholders could not complain of unfairness. Lord Simmonds (whose judgment formed the majority view) likened a preference shareholder to a creditor and said that such a person ought to expect that, in return for the extra degree of security and lower risk that his investment carried, he must appreciate that the company can, on a reduction of its capital, lawfully pay him back at any time just as it can repay a loan.

Re Floating Dock of St Thomas Ltd (1895)

The company had three classes of shares – first preference shares, second preference shares and ordinary shares. The first and second preference shares had rights to repayment of the nominal value of their shares in that order of priority and the ordinary shareholders had rights to any surplus capital. The company's major asset was a floating dock on the Thames and when it sank to the bottom of the river a major capital loss occurred so a reduction of capital scheme was proposed. The scheme would cancel all the ordinary shares and all the second preference shares and would reduce the nominal value of the first preference shares by £1 each. Some of the second preference shareholders objected to the proposed reduction.

Held Where there is a loss of capital and this has to be borne by a reduction of capital scheme then the reduction should mirror what would have happened in an insolvent winding up of that company. The class of shares which would first lose rights to capital repayment (in this case the ordinary shareholders followed by the second preference shares) should be the first to bear the loss in a reduction of capital too.

Re Chatterley-Whitfield Collieries Ltd (1948) CA

The company had two classes of shares – ordinary and preference shares (these had priority rights as to dividend and as to repayment of capital in a winding up). The company's colliery business having been nationalised it had more capital than it needed and was proposing a scheme of reduction which would repay and cancel the preference shares. Some of the preference shareholders objected that the scheme was unfair.

Held The scheme was confirmed. Lord Greene MR sending a clear message to preference shareholders

> ... the risk of a reduction of capital taking place is as much an element in the bargain as the right to a preferential dividend, and ... the well-known practice of the courts involves what ... is really in accordance with sound business practice and, moreover, is based on the recognised analogy of priorities as to capital in a winding up, *viz* that, at any rate where preference shares are not entitled to participate in surplus assets, they are to be paid off first on a reduction, and references to the reasonable expectations of preference shareholders which are intended to suggest that there is something inequitable in this form of treatment, have, in my judgment, no support either in practice or on principle, and are unsound.

11.2.3 When is a reduction of capital also a variation of class rights?

Re Welsbach Incandescent Gas Co (1904)

Preference shareholders who were threatened with being repaid early and cancelled by a reduction of capital scheme objected to it, arguing that, as well as being unfair, it was also an abrogation of their class rights within s 125 of the Companies Act (CA) 1985 and they were, accordingly, entitled to the protection of the statutory provisions on variation of class rights.

Held The court rejected this argument – their literal class rights were unaffected by the reduction, it was their enjoyment of those rights that was affected and that was not the same thing as a variation of the rights themselves.

Re Saltdean Estate Co Ltd (1968)
Preference shareholders attempted to use the variation of class rights provisions to defeat a proposed reduction of capital which would pay them 75p for each 50p nominal value share and cancel them as a class.

Held The court refused the application and confirmed the scheme of reduction. The reduction, the court said, was quite in order – the preference shareholders did not have a collective right which was being abrogated within the meaning of s 125 of the CA 1985. It was inherent in the nature of preference shareholding that priority to capital repayment also carries with it the chance that the share may be paid off early at any time as part of a reduction of capital.

House of Fraser plc v ACGE Investments Ltd (1987) HL
Two preference shareholders objected to a proposed reduction of capital on the grounds that it constituted a variation of their class rights in that it repaid and cancelled the class of preference shares. The preference shares carried with them priority rights as to repayment of capital.

Held The House of Lords approved the reduction saying that it involved an application of the class rights of the preference shares not an abrogation of them. Their lordships approved the Court of Session's statement that 'Abolition or abrogation are not appropriate expressions to describe the situation where a right and its corresponding obligation have been extinguished by performance'.

Re Northern Engineering Industries plc (1994) CA
The company's articles of association contained a clause which stipulated that the rights attaching to the company's preference shares shall be deemed to be varied by a reduction of capital paid up on those shares. The preference shareholders invoked this clause when a scheme of reduction of capital was proposed which would have the effect of eliminating them by repayment.

Held The Court of Appeal upheld their objection and ruled that the proposed reduction fell within the article and the cancellation of the preference shares was thus deemed to be a variation of their rights.

11.3   Section 425 reconstructions

Re Dorman Long (1934)

Dorman Long & Co Ltd reached a provisional agreement with the South Durham Steel and Iron Company Ltd that it should acquire South Durham's business assets and undertaking. Each company prepared a scheme of arrangement between it, its debenture holders and its shareholders in order to sanction the acquisition. The court's approval to the schemes was sought under the then forerunner of s 425 of the CA 1985.

Held Maugham J said that the court had a duty to scrutinise carefully complicated schemes of arrangement and in deciding whether or not to sanction any particular scheme of arrangement the court must be satisfied that the resolutions approving it were passed in compliance with the statutory majority required and that any proposal contained in the scheme is such that intelligent and honest members of the classes concerned would, if they were acting in their own interests, approve.

Re NFU Development Trust Ltd (1973)

The NFU Development Trust Ltd was a company limited by guarantee with no share capital. The NFU Development Co Ltd was one of its members – the other 94,000 members were farmers. It was proposed to reduce the number of members to seven and this achieved an 85% majority of the 1,439 votes cast. When the schemes came before the court for sanction under the then equivalent provision to s 425 of the CA 1985, the objectors challenged the scheme.

Held The statutory language referred to a 'compromise or arrangement' between the company and its members. That implied some element of give and take amongst the different classes of scheme participant. That element was missing here as the scheme amounted to simply an outright expropriation of the rights of members with no compensating advantage. Hence the scheme could not be approved under the Act.

12 Insider dealing and takeovers

12.1 Insider dealing

12.1.1 The criminal offence

Attorney General's Reference (No 1 of 1988) HL
This was a reference on a point of law arising out of the acquittal of the defendant on a charge of insider dealing under the Company Securities (Insider Dealing) Act (CS(ID)A) 1985. The defendant had sought to buy a block of shares in a public company but negotiations with the vendors had fallen through and the deal was off. An employee of the merchant bank advising the vendors told the defendant that the vendors were selling to another named party and that that, in itself, was confidential price-sensitive information because this deal had not yet been made public. In spite of that warning, the defendant bought shares on the stock market before the public announcement of the sale which he later sold at a profit. At his trial, he argued that there was no case to answer since he did not 'obtain' any information from the merchant bank's employee; the CS(ID)A 1985 required secondary insiders (tippees) to have obtained the inside information from a primary insider, which he argued imported some more active element than was present in this case – he merely passively received the information – it was freely volunteered to him.

Held Whereas the trial judge agreed with the defendant's interpretation of the word obtain (hence his acquittal), both the Court of Appeal and the House of Lords were of the view that a person obtains inside information for the purposes of the Act (and thus falls within its ambit) even if he did not solicit the inside information and came by it without any positive action on his behalf. Lord Templeman said: 'The object of the [Insider Dealing] Act was to prevent insider dealing. Parliament cannot have intended that a man who asks for information which he then misuses should be convicted of an offence ... while a man who, without asking, learns the same information which he also misuses should be acquitted.'

(Although of interest in showing how this relatively young criminal offence is evolving in the courts it is not strictly relevant now as the 1985 legislation has been replaced by Part V of the Criminal Justice Act 1993, which implements the EC Directive on Insider Dealing 89/52/EEC, and s 57(2)(b) of that Act uses the phrase 'has information from an inside source' to characterise a secondary insider and so puts the issue raised in this case beyond doubt now.)

12.1.2 Defences

R v Cross (1991)
The defendant left the board of directors of a company about which he possessed inside information. As part of his severance package from the company he took up shares in it under the terms of the company's share option scheme. He then sold them almost immediately and when charged with the offence of insider dealing as a result he argued in his defence that it was his belief that it was a term of the share option scheme that he had to sell his shares within 30 days otherwise he would have lost all rights to them, that was his motive for selling the shares not the 'making or profit or avoiding of a loss' (the *mens rea* required by the CS(ID)A 1985). He argued that, had he believed he had a free choice in the matter, he would have retained the shares and not sold them. Hence, he argued, he lacked the necessary *mens rea*.

Held The Court of Criminal Appeal said that in order to rely successfully on this defence, because the matters pertinent to making it out were peculiarly within the defendant's knowledge, the onus of proof was on the defendant to prove, on the balance of probabilities, that he fell within this defence. (Section 53(1)(c) of the Criminal Justice Act 1993 makes this clearer now too.)

12.1.3 Enforcement

Re an Inquiry under the Company Securities (Insider Dealing) Act 1985 (1988) HL
A business journalist had written two articles which accurately predicted decisions on the legality of proposed mergers of the Monopolies and Mergers Commission before they were publicly announced. This suggested a leak or leaks within either a governmental body or department and inspectors were appointed under s 177 of the Financial Services Act (FSA) 1986 to investigate. They summoned the journalist to answer questions as to where he got the information (as s 177 entitled them to do) but he refused to name his source or sources, arguing that he could not be held to be in any contempt as journalists enjoyed a special privilege to protect their sources.

Held The judge at first instance held that the inspectors' s 177 power to investigate insider dealing was subject to that excuse from the law of contempt. However, both the Court of Appeal and the House of Lords disagreed. They thought the only relevance of the journalist's assertion to be entitled to public interest immunity in his refusal to name his sources was that it meant the burden of proof to show that the identification of the sources was necessary for the prevention of crime was on the inspectors. They did not, however, have to show that the information sought was necessary for the prevention of any specific crime of insider dealing, it was enough that they show that the situation was such that the information sought was needed for the detection and deterrence of insider dealing crime generally. So if there was leakiness within government bodies or departments which were giving out inside information, which might in turn lead to the offence of insider dealing taking place then that was sufficient justification for the exercise of the s 177 of the FSA 1986 power to question. Indeed, stamping out insider dealing was the whole point of introducing this tough investigatory power to compel the disclosure of information.

12.2 Takeovers

12.2.1 The Takeover Panel

R v Panel on Takeovers and Mergers ex parte Datafin plc (1987) CA
Datafin plc brought an application for judicial review of decisions and procedures of the Takeover Panel, that arose out of its contested bid for Norton Opax. It was the first time a court had ever considered the status, role and actions of the Takeover Panel and it was unclear whether it, as a private self regulatory body, was subject to the public law jurisdiction of judicial review

Held The Court of Appeal held that the Panel's decisions were capable of being subject to judicial review but because of the special environment in which the Panel acted and the need for certainty, speed and finality in its decision making any relief a court may give would be limited to 'ex post' declaratory relief only. This would preserve the benefits and flexibility of self-regulation. In reaching his conclusion that decisions of the the Panel were, in principle, judicially reviewable, Lord Donaldson MR said:

> [The Panel] is without doubt performing a public duty and an important one. This is clear from the expressed willingness of the Secretary of State for Trade and Industry to limit legislation in the field of takeovers and mergers and to use the panel s the centrepiece of his regulation of that market. The rights of citizens are indirectly affected by its decisions ... At least in its determination of whether there has been breach of the Code it has a duty to act judicially and it asserts that its *raison d'etre* is to do equity between one shareholder and another. Its source of power is only partly based on moral persuasion and the assent of institutions and their members, the bottom line being the statutory powers exercised by the

[DTI] and the Bank of England. In this context, I should be very disappointed if the courts could not recognise the realities of executive power and allow their vision to be clouded by the subtlety and sometimes complexity of the way in which it can exerted ...

He made clear that he did not wish to fetter or hamper in any way the Panel's efficacy and/or open the floodgates to nuisance/tactical litigation during the course of a takeover bid, hence the Court of Appeal's decision to limit the relief available to declaratory orders once a bid is concluded.

R v Panel on Takeovers and Mergers ex parte Guinness plc (1989) CA

The Panel announced that it would investigate whether or not Guinness had been acting in concert with another person during its contested takeover bid for Distillers at the same time as a DTI inquiry into Guinness conduct of the bid was still in progress. Guinness objected to the Panel's refusal to adjourn its inquiries pending the outcome of the DTI inquiry and applied for judicial review.

Held With a body as unusual as the Takeover Panel, it was necessary to consider the question of whether something had gone wrong with the fairness of its procedures as a whole and the court felt that overall the Panel's investigation of Guinness had been fair and no injustice was caused. The decision of whether or not to grant adjournments involved the exercise of a judicial discretion by the Panel, and the Panel's own procedures granted a right of appeal from such decisions which Guinness had chosen not to exercise. In such circumstances, a court would only very exceptionally intervene by way of judicial review.

R v Panel on Takeovers and Mergers ex parte Fayed (1992) CA

Mr Al Fayed and others, who had launched a successful takeover bid for House of Fraser (including most famously Harrods store) in 1985 now sought a judicial review of the Takeover Panel's decision to bring disciplinary proceedings against them relating to their conduct in the course of that bid. The decision to bring disciplinary proceedings was based on the findings of a 1991 DTI report into the bid which criticised the applicants. The applicants argued that the Panel should not just rely on this report but should make its own investigation and also, that any disciplinary proceedings should be stayed until after the hearing of civil action against them by Lonrho plc (the loser in the 1985 contested bid for House of Fraser).

Held Judicial review was refused – there was no threat of prejudice to the Lonrho civil action and Panel disciplinary proceedings could be based on a DTI report without there necessarily being unfairness. Unless an applicant could show fraud or bad faith, a court would not intervene on the question of whether grounds existed for the bringing of disciplinary proceedings by the Panel.

12.2.2 Directors' duties on a takeover

Re a Company (1986)

A private company was subject to two rival takeover bids. One of the bidding companies was controlled by the target company's directors (this bid was referred to in the case as the 'N bid'). The other bid, which was for a higher price, was being made by a trade competitor of the target company. The target company's chairman had sent a circular to all shareholders of the target company urging them to accept the N bid and detailing reasons why the higher bid would be unsuccessful. A s 459 petition was brought alleging that the target company's directors had breached their duty in failing to recommend the higher priced bid and in failing to take steps to tenure the success of that bid and this breach constituted unfair prejudice.

Held Hoffmann J said that a target company's directors were not under a positive duty to recommend and do all within their power to ensure that the highest takeover offer succeeded, their duty only extended to the duty to act fairly so as to enable shareholders to reach an informed decision by giving them sufficient information and not misleading them or hampering their ability to accept the better priced bid. In this particular case, however, he allowed the s 459 action to continue as the chairman's circular was capable of misleading the shareholder recipients.

Dawson International plc v Coats Paton plc (1988) Court of Session

Lord Cullen, sitting in the Outer House of the Scottish Court of Session, said that he could envisage circumstances where a company would have a legitimate interest in any change in the identity of it shareholders, one bid may be in the interest of the company and another may not. However, directors were not under any fiduciary duty to shareholders, and were certainly not under any such duty to current shareholders in respect of advising or enabling them to sell their shares for the best possible price. Although directors were under a duty to consider the interests of shareholder as they went about discharging their duties to the company, that was not the same thing as considering the interests of shareholders as sellers of their shares. He said: 'What is in the interests of current shareholders as sellers of their shares may not necessarily coincide with what is in the interests of the company.' Of course, if directors do decide to advise shareholders in their capacity as targets of offers to have their shares bought, then they must not mislead them and must act in good faith; if they fail to do so, they will be liable to those shareholders but that is not the converse of any pre-existing general fiduciary duty owed directly to shareholders in this context.

Hogg v Cramphorn Ltd (1966)
See Chapter 5, above, 5.4.3.

Gething v Kilner (1972)
Town Centre Securities Ltd made an offer for the issued share capital of the Rochdale Canal Co, offering £200 for every £100 of stock held. The board of directors of Rochdale recommended the offer for acceptance to their shareholders and some acceptances were received. However, the plaintiff (a shareholder in Rochdale) brought an action seeking an injunction to prevent Town Centre Ltd's offer proceeding and being declared unconditional.

Held The interlocutory relief sought was not granted, the judge being satisfied that the Rochdale directors acted honestly and reasonably in making their recommendation of acceptance. He said: 'I accept that the directors of an offeree company have a duty towards their own shareholders, which in my view clearly includes a duty to be honest and not to mislead.'

Heron International Ltd v Lord Grade (1983) CA
The facts of this case were unusual as the company which was the target of two rival takeover bids (referred to in the case as 'Bell' and 'Heron') had a special article of association which provided that the transfer of any voting share in the company could only be made to a person nominated by the directors and such transfer must be approved by the Independent Broadcasting Authority. It was alleged that the target's directors had acted unreasonably and in breach of their duty in deciding that the Bell bid should be accepted.

Held Lord Justice Lawton, giving the judgment of the court, emphasised the fiduciary nature of the directors' power under the special article and said: 'Where the directors have decided that it is in the interests of the company that the company should be taken over, and where there are two or more bidders, the only duty of the directors, who have powers such as those contained in [the special article], is to obtain the best price ... the interests of the company must be the interests of the current shareholders.'

12.2.3 Sections 428–30F of the Companies Act 1985

Re Carlton Holdings (1971)
The terms of a takeover offer which had proved successful had originally included a cash alternative but this was not offered to the non-accepting minority shareholders when they were being bought out under the statutory provisions for the compulsory acquisition of a 10% minority.

Held This was wrong – the minority being subject to a compulsory acquisition must be offered precisely the same terms as the original takeover offer which had been accepted by the 90% majority of the shareholders, in this case that meant a cash alternative must be offered too.

Re Bugle Press Ltd (1960) CA

The majority shareholders in Bugle Press Ltd, J and S (who between them owned 90% of the shares) attempted to use the compulsory acquisition of a minority provisions to oust the 10% minority shareholder, T, from Bugle Press Ltd. J and S formed a £100 company – J & S Holdings Ltd – which then made a takeover offer to Bugle Press Ltd's shareholders at £10 per share. Obviously, J and S accepted this offer, T refused it saying the price was too low, and so J & S Holdings Ltd attempted to squeeze T out by exercising its statutory right to buy him out under the forerunner of s 429 of the Companies Act (CA) 1985.

Held The attempted squeeze-out failed. Lord Evershed MR examined the rationale for the compulsory acquisition provisions and said '... what the section is directed to is a case where there is a scheme or contract for the acquisition of a company, its amalgamation, reorganisation or the like, and where the offeror is independent of the shareholders in the transferor company or of that part of fraction of them from which the 90% is to be derived ...'. He left open the possibility, however, that the provisions could be invoked in this way if it could be shown that there was a good reason in the interests of the company to so do, and he gave as an example the situation where the minority shareholder 'was in some way acting in a manner destructive or highly damaging to the interests of the company from some motives entirely of his own'.

Chez Nico (Restaurants) Ltd (1992)

Some of the company's shareholders tried to use ss 428ff of the CA 1985 to buy out the others. They sent letters to the minority shareholders which invited them to offer their shares for sale.

Held Sections 428ff did not apply because the bidding shareholders had merely sent out an invitation to treat and not an offer to purchase the shares of the minority. The court also said that even where a takeover bidder was a private company, and hence not subject to the City Code on Takeovers and Mergers, a court could still take account of the extent and nature of disclosure made by a bidder to shareholders and whether or not it complied with City Code standards.

13 Charges

13.1 Fixed and floating charges

Re Yorkshire Woolcombers Association Ltd (1903) CA

Romer LJ said that a floating charge had three key characteristics:

- It is a charge on a class of assets of the company which includes present and future assets.
- The composition of the class is not fixed – it changes from time to time in the ordinary course of the company's business.
- The charge contemplates that the company is free to carry on business normally and deal with the assets subject to it in the ordinary course of that business until such time as the charge holders enforce the charge – so it 'floats' in suspense until that time.

Re Panama, New Zealand and Australian Royal Mail Co (1870) CA

The instrument creating the charge had purported to charge the whole undertaking and the question arose as to what this term included – could it include all the property of the company that was being realised now that the company was being wound up?

Held Lord Justice Giffard said '... under these debentures, they have a charge upon all property of the company, past and future, by the term "undertaking", and that they stand in a position superior to that of the general creditors who can touch nothing until they are paid'. Thus, it was established that a floating charge can operate over the whole of a company's undertaking. It need not specify a particular class or classes of assets.

Siebe Gorman & Co Ltd v Barclays Bank Ltd (1979)

A company created a debenture secured over its present and future book debts. The question arose – was it a fixed or a floating charge?

Held Slade J characterised this charge as a fixed charge. He said that, although it was more usual for a charge over book debts to be a floating charge, this particular charge had the characteristics of a fixed charge since, once the company had received the moneys in payment of its book debts, it was not then free to deal with it as it liked but was subject to a requirement in the charge instrument to pay it into the company's account at the chargeholder bank.

Re New Bullas Trading Ltd (1993) CA

This case concerned a hybrid type of charge – was it fixed or floating? The company had sought to grant a fixed charge over its book debts, the chargee was entitled to have the debts assigned to it if it so required. It was also entitled to direct as to how the company should deal with its book debts. The proceeds of the debts were to be paid into a bank account designated by the chargee and only if the chargee failed to give any directions as to how any moneys paid in should be dealt with would the company then be free to deal with the moneys as it wished. What the parties had clearly tried to do was to create a fixed charge over the book debts and moneys arising from them. This allowed for the possibility for the moneys 'leaving' the scope of the fixed charge if it was not 'activated' by the chargee and becoming subject to the company's floating charge. The administrative receiver asked the court to characterise this charge. The court at first instance called it a floating charge.

Held The Court of Appeal upheld the primacy of freedom of contract in the context of creation of charges and said that this was indeed a fixed charge over the book debts whilst uncollected, and a floating charge over the proceeds of such debts once they had been paid into the designated bank account.

Re GE Tunbridge Ltd (1995)

The question arose, during the administration of the company, as to the status of a charge it had created over its assets in the following terms: the debenture sought to charge 'All other assets (not being floating assets) now owned or hereafter acquired by the [Company] – or in which it now has or in the future acquires an interest'. Floating assets were defined elsewhere in the charge so the parties clearly thought they were creating a fixed charge – but were they?

Held No – this definition of assets charged created a floating charge. Sir Mervyn Davies concluded that the document read as a whole disclosed a floating charge despite what the parties to it may have contemplated. He found that the three characteristics that Romer LJ identified in *Yorkshire Woolcombers* were all present and this overrode the parties' stated contrary intention.

Re Cimex Tissues Ltd (1995)

The company concerned was a toilet paper manufacturer which had purported to issue a fixed charge over its machinery pursuant to which it had agreed not to sell, mortgage, or otherwise deal with the charged property, other than in the ordinary course of its trading business, without the prior written consent of the lender.

Held This was a fixed charge – the restriction on the company's right to deal as it liked with the charged property clearly gave it the characteristics of a fixed charge. The judge said:

> The authorities on floating charges to which I have been referred do not lead me to conclude that, in the case of a charge over specific manufacturing machinery, a liberty for the chargor to deal to some extent with that machinery without the consent of the chargee is necessarily inconsistent with the creation of a fixed charge.

Royal Trust Bank v National Westminster Bank plc (1994) CA

An equipment hire and leasing company executed deeds of assignment and a charge in favour of Royal Trust Bank (RTB) in exchange for a banking facility. The charge purported to create a fixed charge over hiring agreements on deposit at RTB and the proceeds of such agreements. Moneys due under the agreements were to be collected by the company as agents for RTB, and the company could be required by RTB to open a special 'rental income collection account' for such moneys. In fact, no such account was ever required to be opened and the relevant moneys were simply paid into the company's bank account at National Westminster Bank (the existence of this account pre-dated the charge agreement). From time to time, payment was made to RTB out of the Nat West account until 1992 when Nat West stopped further payment. RTB brought an action against Nat West claiming it was a constructive trustee of moneys which belonged in equity to RTB because they were the subject of the equitable fixed charge. Nat West conceded that the charge was a fixed and not a floating charge before the case went to the Court of Appeal.

Held Despite Nat West's concession as to the nature of the charge, Millet LJ disagreed and said that he thought the charge was properly characterised as a floating charge (although this, of course, is purely *obiter*). He said:

> The proper characterisation of a security as 'fixed' or 'floating' depends on the freedom of the chargor to deal with the proceeds of the charged assets in the ordinary course of business free from the security. A contractual right in the chargor to collect the proceeds and pay them into its own bank account for use in the ordinary course of its business is a badge of a floating charge and is inconsistent with the existence of a fixed charge: see *Re Brightlife*. I would therefore ... notwithstanding the concession made by National Westminster before us, characterise the charge created [in this case] as a floating charge, notice of the existence of which would not affect the priority of Nat West's rights in respect of the moneys in the account.

13.2 Priorities as between charges

Wheatley v Silkstone and Haigh Moor Coal Company (1885)

The company had issued in 1878 a floating charge over its whole undertaking, lands, mines, cottages, revenue and other effects both present and future. This was expressed to be a 'first charge' on the property subject to it. In 1881, the company borrowed money from the plaintiff in return for an equitable mortgage by way of deposit of lease and title deeds of a colliery. The company agreed that it would execute a legal mortgage over this property should the plaintiff ever request it to do so.

The question for the court was – which charge had priority?

Held A subsequent fixed charge (legal or equitable) over specific assets has priority over an earlier floating charge.

Re Benjamin Cope & Sons Ltd (1914)

The company had issued one set of debentures secured by a floating charge in 1894 and a second subsequent set in 1904. The question before the court was – which took priority, or were they all to be ranked *pari passu*?

Held The first debentures had priority over the second. Sargant J said:

> ... generally speaking, it would in my view be as incompatible with the company's bargain with the first debenture holders to put their debentures behind or on the same footing as subsequent debentures giving a charge of the same character, as if the debentures had constituted a specific charge and it were then attempted to create a subsequent specific charge ranking *pari passu* with them or in priority to them.

Re Automatic Bottle Makers (1926)

A debenture was issued on 15 January 1925. The company reserved the right to create a later charge ranking in priority over an earlier one or *pari passu*. A second debenture was then issued on 11 August 1925 which was to take advantage of the reservation by the company.

Held The court held that it was perfectly possible to change the usual order of priority, ie first in time first in right, if the contracting parties wished so to do.

13.3 Crystallisation of floating charges

13.3.1 Floating charges crystallise when the company no longer carries on its business, when security is enforced or when winding up commences

Re Woodroffes (Musical Instruments) Ltd (1986)

The company created two floating charges, one in favour of the bank and the other in favour of Mrs Woodroffe. The latter charge contained a clause stating that Mrs Woodroffe could change her charge into a fixed charge by giving the requisite notice. This she did on 27 August 1982. Receivers were appointed on 1 September 1982. The question was which charge took priority?

Held Mrs Woodroffe's charge ranked before the bank's. The notice given by Mrs Woodroffe did not have the effect of crystallising the bank's charge.

N W Robbie & Co Ltd v Whitney Warehouse Co Ltd (1963) CA

The plaintiff company had issued a floating charge to a bank. The bank appointed a receiver in order to enforce the charge and to this end the receiver continued to carry on the company's business. The defendants bought goods from the company. When the receiver claimed payment of the purchase price, the defendants claimed to be able to set-off their liability to pay, against a debt due from the company.

Held Since the floating charge had 'ceased to float' or had crystallised when the receiver was appointed, the debt owed by the defendants became a chose in action subject to the floating charge in favour of the bank, and the defendants were not thus entitled to any set-off.

Re Crompton & Co (1914)

In 1895 the company issued debentures secured by a floating charge over all the assets of the company. The terms of the charge provided that the principal lent should become immediately repayable (*inter alia*) if a winding up order was made or a resolution was passed to wind up the company, save for the purposes of reconstruction, reorganisation or amalgamation. In 1913 a resolution for the purposes of reconstruction of the company was passed whereby its assets were transferred to a new company formed expressly for that purpose. The debenture holders applied to court for the appointment of a receiver to enforce their security.

Held Notwithstanding the provision in the charge, the floating charge crystallised as soon as the old company was wound up, and the security it provided was enforceable. Thus the plaintiffs could appoint a receiver.

13.3.2 Effects of automatic crystallisation

Re Brightlife Ltd (1986)

Brightlife Ltd went into creditor's voluntary liquidation owing £200,000, secured by debenture to Norandex, and £70,000 to the Commissioners of Customs and Excise, who are classed as preferential creditors. A clause in the debenture stipulated that the chargee could crystallise the floating charge, if it was believed the security was in jeopardy. The liquidator wanted guidance as to the effectiveness of the clause.

Held The court stated that crystallisation was possible in this instance and consequently the debenture holder did not have to wait until the preferential creditors were paid. Mr Justice Hoffmann was urged to consider the prejudice to other creditors that the operation of automatic crystallisation clauses could cause. However, he rejected this consideration saying:

> I do not think that it is open to the courts to restrict the contractual freedom of parties to a floating charge on such grounds. The floating charge was invented by Victorian lawyers to enable manufacturing and trading companies to raise loan capital on debentures. It could offer the security of a charge over the whole of the company's undertaking without inhibiting its ability to trade. But the mirror image of these advantages was the potential prejudice to the general body of creditors, who might know nothing of the floating charge but find that all the company's assets, including the very goods which they had just delivered on credit, had been swept up by the debenture holder. The public interest requires a balancing of the advantages to the economy of facilitating the borrowing of money against the possibility of injustice to unsecured creditors. These arguments for and against floating charges are matters for Parliament rather than the courts ...

13.4 Registration of charges

13.4.1 What happens when the information on the register is wrong?

Re Eric Holmes (1965)
A debenture in favour of Mr Richards was executed by the firm on 5 June. The documentation was sent to the company solicitors, but without a date on it. The solicitors were in a state of disarray at the time because the active partner had been killed. The date on the documentation was filled in as 23 June, which would have been within the 21 day period for registration. Evidently, if the true date of execution was used, the charge had not been registered within time. A certificate was issued by Companies House stating the requirements of the Act had been complied with.

Held The charge was valid. Section 98(2) of the Companies Act (CA) 1948 states that a certificate is conclusive evidence that the requirements of the act have been complied with. (Now s 401 of the CA 1985.)

13.4.2 Registration out of time, s 404(1) and (2)

Re Telomatic (1994)
A charge was created by Barclays Bank over land owned by Telomatic. The charge was dated 4 January, but was not registered at Companies House at that time. The bank realised the charge had not been registered on 4

October and tried three times to procure security for their charge. On 5 October, the Cyprus Bank took a second charge over the property. Barclays Bank then applied to the court to get rectification of the register.

Held Registration out of time was not granted by the court. First, Barclays had misled the court as to whether the company was to be wound up. Secondly, Barclays had tried to procure security in several ways before attempting to use s 404. Registration out of time will normally be granted, but it was held to be inequitable to do so in this instance.

13.5 Retention of title clauses

13.5.1 Validity of clauses

Aluminium Industrie Vaassen BV v Romalpa Aluminium Ltd (1976) CA
A Dutch company supplied aluminium foil to an English company. The contract between them contained a retention of title clause, which stated that legal title to the foil did not pass to the English company until full payment had been made. Anything made from the foil was to be held by the company as bailees and was to be kept separately from any other manufactured goods. The company was entitled to deal in the ordinary course of business with any products manufactured, but in such a case the company was acting as the agent of the supplier.

Held The clause was effective. The suppliers could claim any aluminium still in its original form, and they could trace into any proceeds of sale from goods manufactured from their aluminium.

Re Bond Worth (1990)
Raw fibre was sold to Bond Worth who manufactured carpets. An attempt to create a valid retention of title clause was made by reserving 'equitable and beneficial ownership' in the fibre, until payment had been made. No mention of retaining the legal title was made.

Held The clause was held to be a floating charge because only equitable title had been retained by the supplier. Consequently, since the charge had not been registered, it was void and so the suppliers could not claim their goods back.

13.5.2 What happens when the goods are no longer in their original form?

Re Peachdart (1981)
Leather was supplied to Peachdart, a company who made handbags. A retention of title clause was included in the terms of the contract, stating that the suppliers retained ownership in the leather and anything manufactured from it, until payment was made. The leather was in various

stages of manufacture when the company went into liquidation, some pieces of leather were simply cut ready to make into handbags, other pieces were already made up into the finished articles. The supplier attempted to claim that he had a right to the cut leather and the handbags.

Held The court stated that the leather had entered the manufacturing process and so it was no longer identifiable. Hence, the supplier was not successful in his claim.

Hendy Lennox v Puttick Ltd (1984)

Diesel engines were supplied to Puttick Ltd. A retention of title clause was included in the contract which reserved title to the engines until they were paid for. They were then fitted into generating sets for customers of Puttick. Puttick then went into receivership. Two out of three generating sets were in a deliverable state and therefore could not be claimed by the supplier. The third was not in a deliverable state and remained identifiable because of its serial number.

Held The third generating set could be claimed by the supplier because it was identifiable and not in a deliverable state.

14 Liquidation and the Insolvency Act 1986

14.1 Purpose of liquidation

British Eagle International Airlines Ltd v Compagnie Nationale Air France (1975) HL

A number of international air carriers had established a clearing house arrangement with the International Air Transport Association which was designed to operate a collectivised netting-off arrangement of monies owing between all the members. This had the effect that no one airline claimed monies from another but a monthly balance owing each one was paid by the clearing house. When the plaintiff company went into liquidation and the liquidator claimed monies allegedly owing it from the defendant company, the question arose as to the validity of the clearing house arrangement in the context of a liquidation. Could such a mechanism take precedence over the statutorily ordained rules on company liquidations?

Held Section 302 of the Companies Act (CA) 1948 states:

> Subject to the provisions of this Act as to preferential payments, the property of a company, shall on its winding up, be applied in satisfaction of its liabilities *pari passu*, and, subject to such application, shall, unless the articles otherwise provide, be distributed among the members according to their rights and interests in the company.

That is the essence and fundamental purpose of the rules on company liquidation and so, in as much as it sought to contract out of s 302 of the CA 1948 [now s 107 of the Insolvency Act (IA) 1986] this clearing house arrangement for the payment of debts was void and contrary to public policy. Lord Cross said:

> The question is, in essence, whether what was called in argument the 'mini liquidation' flowing from the clearing house arrangement is to yield to or to prevail over the general liquidation. I cannot doubt that on principle the rules of the general liquidation should prevail.

14.2 Duties of a liquidator

Re Armstrong Whitworth Securities Ltd (1947)

From 1896 the company carried on an engineering business. From 1918 until 1933, the company kept records of accidents in the work place which involved their employees when the company insured against such accidents. The liquidator advertised for any creditors to come forward when the company went into liquidation in September 1943, but did not have regard to the records kept by the company of accidents and their victims.

Held The liquidator had not fulfilled his duties, he had a duty to contact all known creditors. He should have made use of the company records when working out who were creditors of the company.

14.3 Fraudulent trading: s 213

14.3.1 What constitutes fraudulent trading?

Re Maidstone Buildings Provisions Ltd (1971)

Mr Penney was the secretary for the company and not a director. Debts were incurred by the company when it was evident the company was insolvent.

Held The person concerned must take an active part in the fraudulent trading to be liable under this section. The fact that the secretary of the company warned the other directors that they should stop trading was not enough to render those directors liable for fraudulent trading.

Re Gerald Cooper Chemicals Ltd (1978)

A loan was made by J to C Ltd. The company subsequently became insolvent. H then paid C Ltd, in advance, for some indigo dye. The dye was never delivered and the money advanced was used to pay off part of the loan made by J.

Held The single transaction could amount to fraudulent trading.

Re Sarflax Ltd (1979)

The company entered into a contract with another called SAFE, to deliver a type of press. It did not work and SAFE attempted to rescind the contract, claiming £80,000 plus interest. The company then went into liquidation. Company assets were sold to discharge debts, but the debt owed to SAFE was disregarded.

Held The fact that the transaction entered into gave one creditor an advantage over another was not evidence of fraudulent trading.

14.3.2 Must the officer have knowledge of the fraudulent trading?

Re William Leitch Brothers (No 1) (1932)

The company was incorporated in December 1926. By the end of 1929 the company was in serious financial difficulties, and by 30 March 1930 the company was unable to pay its debts. William Leitch, a director of the firm, knew that the company owed £6,500 and would not be able to pay it. However, he proceeded to borrow a further £6,000. In June of that year, the company was wound up and the liquidator wanted the court to find Mr Leitch personally liable for the debts of the company.

Held Mr Leitch was found guilty of fraudulent trading. The test should be subjective, ie what was the knowledge of the particular director at the time? In other words, the court is not concerned with the question of what a reasonable director would have believed had he been in the same position.

Re Patrick & Lyon Ltd (1933)

The case concerned the meaning of s 275 of the CA 1929 which provided that:

> If in the course of the winding up of a company it appears that any business of the company has been carried on with intent to defraud creditors of the company or ... for any fraudulent purpose, the court, on the application of ... the liquidator or any creditor or contributory ... may declare that any of the directors ... of the company who were knowingly parties to the carrying on of the business in manner aforesaid shall be personally responsible, without any limitation of liability, for all or any of the debts of the company as the court may direct.

That section was the forerunner of the modern s 216 of the IA 1986 and so what the court had to say then is still of relevance today.

Held The phrases 'intent to defraud' and 'fraudulent purpose' implied that actual dishonesty must be present as an element rather than fraud in the equitable sense. Maugham J said:

> [These] words connote actual dishonesty involving, according to current notions of fair trading among commercial men, real moral blame. No judge, I think, has ever been willing to define 'fraud' and I am attempting no definition.

14.3.3 Remedies

Re Cyona Distribution (1967)

In this case it was established that a director was guilty of fraudulent trading. The question before the court was what remedy was available to the creditors.

Held Punitive and/or exemplary damages could be awarded.

14.4 Wrongful trading: s 214

14.4.1 What constitutes wrongful trading?

Re Produce Marketing Consortium Ltd (1989)

Two directors were running a fruit importing business and continued to do so when they ought to have known that there was no chance of the company remaining solvent.

Held They were liable under s 214 for wrongful trading. Although the two directors did not know that the company was in a grave financial situation and about to become insolvent, Knox J stated that that was immaterial. Under s 214 there is a objective test and the directors will be judged not just on what information they had but any information that, 'given reasonable diligence and an appropriate level of general knowledge, skill and experience, was ascertainable.'

Re DKG Contractors Ltd (1990)

Two directors of a groundswork company were consistently failing to have any regard to the Companies Acts, although they were never dishonest. The company then collapsed.

Held The directors were guilty of wrongful trading and had to contribute £500,000 towards the company's debts.

Re Purpoint Ltd (1990) BCLC 491

The difficulty here was deciding when s 214 liability should date from – as no proper company records where kept. When should it have been plain to the director concerned that the company could not avoid going into insolvent liquidation? It was emphasised again that the purpose of an order under s 214 is to recoup the loss to the company so as to benefit all of the company's creditors – the court has no jurisdiction to direct payment to a particular class of creditor or creditors.

Norman v Theodore Goddard (1991)

For facts, see 6.2 above. Hoffmann J, in discussing a company director's common law duty of care and skill, said:

... a director performing active duties on behalf of the company need not exhibit a greater degree of skill than may reasonably be expected from a person undertaking those duties. A director who undertakes the management of the company's properties is expected to have reasonable skill in property management, but not in offshore tax avoidance. It may be that in considering what a director ought reasonably to have known or inferred, one should also take into account the knowledge, skill and experience which he actually had in addition to that which a person carrying out his functions should be expected to have ...

He went on to approve s 214(4) of the IA 1986 as being an accurate statement of the extent of a director's duty of care and skill.

Re Sherborne Associates Ltd (1994)

This case concerned an application by the company's liquidator under s 214 against three of the company's non-executive directors for an order that they contribute personally to the company's assets. The company was an advertising agency that went into insolvent liquidation with a shortfall of over £100,000 in February 1989. The three directors concerned in this action had all resigned from the board in December 1988. The liquidator, however, argued that by specified dates in January 1988 the directors ought to have concluded that there was in fact no reasonable prospect of the company being able to avoid insolvent liquidation. One of the directors died before the liquidator's application was heard and his personal representatives argued that any claim the liquidator might have against him under s 214 was extinguished on his death, so that his estate would be under no liability to contribute to the company's assets even if the wrongful trading case against him were made out.

Held The court said that since the purpose of s 214 was compensatory, this was a commercial purpose aimed at restoring a company's wrongfully depleted assets, so there was no reason to conclude Parliament had intended a s 214 claim to be defeated by the death of the relevant director. However, on the facts of this case, the allegation of wrongful trading was not made out and the court counselled against the dangers of being overly wise and judgmental with the benefit of hindsight.

14.5   Avoidance of a preference: s 239

14.5.1   The security given must be in the interests of the company: s 239

Re MC Bacon Ltd (1990)

MC Bacon had an overdraft facility with the bank, which was unsecured. The main customer of MC Bacon terminated business with them. Two directors then retired and the son of one of them took control of the company. The company then became insolvent and the bank required security on the overdraft. This was granted.

Held The charge was valid and not a preference. The company would not be taken to desire all the necessary consequences of its acts as there were acts a company needed to carry out which were not in its interests, but were an unavoidable price of obtaining a sought after advantage. In other words, for the company to continue to use the overdraft facilities, the bank required security. It may not have been in the interests of the company to grant security, as such, but it was a necessary step to take.

14.6 Avoidance of a floating charge: s 245

14.6.1 Money, goods or services must be supplied 'at the same time as' the charge is created, s 245(3)

Re Power Sharpe Investments (1993) CA
Sharpe advanced money to its subsidiary, Shoe Lace Ltd, over several months. The last advance of £11,500 was on 16 July 1990 . A debenture securing the money was then executed on 24 July 1990.

Held The charge was not valid because it was not created at the same time as the money was supplied. The eight day gap between the last advance and the debenture being issued made the charge invalid.

14.6.2 'Money' must be paid to the company in return for the security: s 245(2)(a)

Re Yeovil Glove (1965) CA
The company went into liquidation. An overdraft with the National Provincial Bank was secured by a floating charge created less than 12 months before. During the currency of the charge, the bank met cheques of £110,000 and received some £111,000. No money was paid to the company.
Held The charge was valid. Although no money was paid to the company, the court treated the bank's acts in meeting the company's cheques as the equivalent.

14.6.3 The money must be intended to benefit the company

Re Matthew Ellis Ltd (1933)
The company was insolvent and obtained a loan from its chairman. He was also a partner in a firm which supplied the company with the majority of its stock. The firm would only supply further stock if past debts were fully paid off. The chairman advanced money to the company stipulating that part should be used to pay off its debts.

Held The charge was valid in respect of the proportion that was used to pay off the debt. The benefit to the company was that without the money advanced by the chairman the company would not be supplied stock and would cease trading.

Re Destone Fabrics (1941)
A floating charge was issued to Z. Money was then paid into the company's bank account by Z. The money was used to pay the directors' fees of

A and B and to pay C, representing an amount guaranteed by him in respect of the company's overdraft.

Held The charge was not valid. The transaction did not benefit the company.

14.6.4 Substituting an unsecured loan for a secured loan

Re GT Whyte & Co Ltd (1983)

Lloyd's Associated Banking Co Ltd, a subsidiary of Lloyd's Bank, advanced money to the company. Sub-mortgages should have been created by Whyte as security, but this was not practicable. Lloyd's had been advised to take security over their loan and so they needed to devise a way to do so. This was achieved by a letter of demand for repayment being sent to Whyte by Labco, whilst at the same time Lloyd's agreed to create another credit facility for the company. Floating charges were taken by Lloyd's as security for the new facility.

Held The charge was not valid because it was not in substance a payment to the company. It is not valid to substitute an unsecured loan for a secured one.

14.7 Transactions at an undervalue: s 238 and transactions defrauding creditors: s 423

Re MC Bacon Ltd

For facts, see above, 14.5.1.

Whilst holding that the granting of the debenture in question did not constitute a transaction within s 238(4) of the IA 1986, Millett J said:

> To come within that paragraph, the transaction must be: (i) entered into by the company; (ii) for a consideration; (iii) the value of which measured in money or money's worth; (vi) is significantly less than the value; (v) also measured in money or money's worth; (vi) of the consideration provided by the company. It requires a comparison to be made between the value obtained by the company for the transaction and the value of consideration provided by the company. Both values must be measurable in money or money's worth and both must be considered from the company's point of view ... The mere creation of a security over a company's assets does not deplete them and does not come within [ss 238(4)]. By charging its assets, the company appropriates them to meet the liabilities due to the secured creditor and adversely affects the rights of other creditors in the event of insolvency. But it does not deplete its assets or diminish their value. It retains the right to redeem and the right to sell or remortgage the charged assets. All it loses is the ability to apply the proceeds otherwise than in satisfaction of the secured debt. That is not something capable of valuation in monetary terms and is not customarily disposed of for value.

Arbuthnot Leasing International Ltd v Havelet (Leasing) Ltd (No 2) (1990)

The plaintiff company, Arbuthnot, applied for the appointment of a receiver of the second defendant company ('Finance') or for an order under s 423 of the IA 1986. Finance was an 'off the shelf' company, which one of the directors of the first defendant company ('Leasing') had transferred all Leasing's business and assets to. However, Leasing had debts owing to Arbuthnot which appointed a receiver over Leasing. Arbuthnot argued that it was entitled to an order under s 423 because the transfer of assets to Finance was motivated by a desire to put those assets out of its reach.

Held The order was granted – the fact that the director's motivation in effecting the transfer may not have been a dishonest one and the fact that it was undertaken pursuant to legal advice did not take the transaction outside the scope of s 423.

Index